truths we tell

STORIES FROM THE YARN STAGE

Curated By **Hilary Trudell**

Production Editing by Julianne Dunn

Photography by Stacy Cox
with the exception of self-portraits by Rhonna-Rose Akama-Makia, Rick Chandler,
Rah Howard, Mark Hotchkiss, and Andrea Toomer.
Sara Brown image by Jeston George
Hilary Trudell back cover image by Britt Hill

Cover design and interior layout by Amy Ashford
Edited by Erin Wood

ISBN: 978-1-944528-15-7
Library of Congress Control Number: 2021944525

Printed in the United States of America

Et Alia Press titles are available at special discounts when purchased in quantity.
For details, email hello@etaliapress.com.

Published in the United States of America by:
Et Alia Press
PO Box 7948
Little Rock, AR 72217

hello@etaliapress.com
etaliapress.com

To all the stories, told and untold, and
to all the storytellers who bring them to light.

TABLE OF CONTENTS

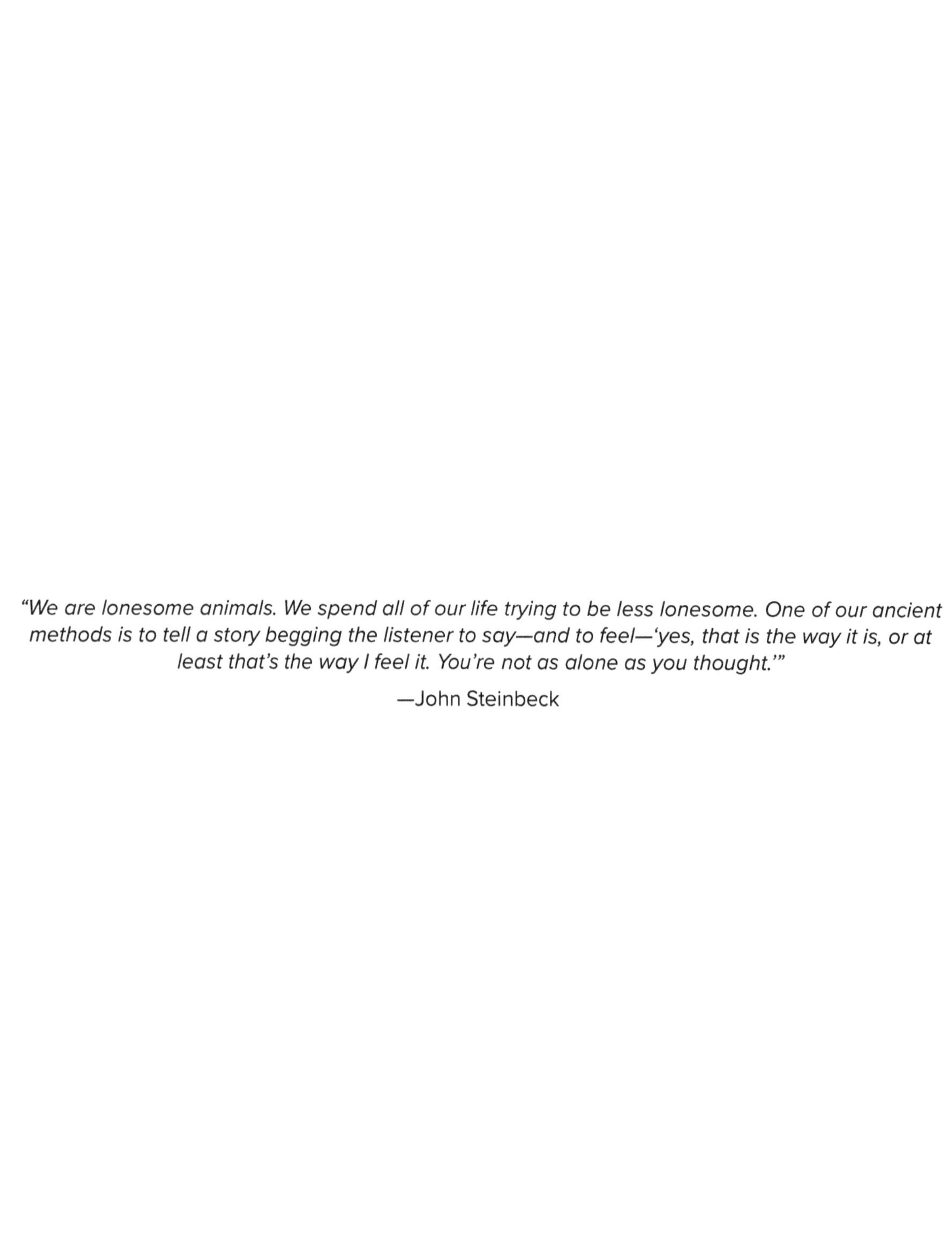

"We are lonesome animals. We spend all of our life trying to be less lonesome. One of our ancient methods is to tell a story begging the listener to say—and to feel—'yes, that is the way it is, or at least that's the way I feel it. You're not as alone as you thought.'"

—John Steinbeck

CURATOR'S INTRODUCTION

When a group of my friends and I decided to start The Yarn, our sole intent was to bring people together. It was 2017, and our country was in a state of intense political division. We were aching to do something, anything, to build bridges (instead of walls) within our small ecosystem. I personally wanted to use my experience as a producer to create a space of empowerment for storytellers and enlightenment for audiences. I was lucky enough to have a team of supportive friends who were willing to try to build something new alongside me.

The original members of The Yarn team were Sara Brown, Jensyn Hallett, Emily Wernsdorfer Hooker, Tiffany Jacob, and Jessi Rice. Omaya D. Jones joined one week after our first show. Our team has evolved over the course of the past four seasons, but the truth is that none of this would have happened without each and every one of them.

Since we took that leap together, The Yarn has served as a platform for over two hundred and fifty storytellers—highlighting the true, lived experiences of Arkansans. We have partnered with many community organizations, listed in the back of this book, to highlight the important work being done in The Natural State. These partnerships have been essential, as our partners have connected us to so many of the storytellers who have graced The Yarn stage.

Our intent with The Yarn was to amplify the voices of those in our community who don't often get the space to speak their truths, and by doing so, shed light on the lived experiences of our neighbors. We hoped that by highlighting these stories, we might broaden our understanding of one another and, in turn, feel a bit more connected. The outpouring of support from the community makes it clear that we had been yearning for this opportunity to relate to one another.

The most incredible thing I have come to witness through this process is the liberating power that sharing a story can bring to the storyteller. When coaching storytellers, I have seen them grapple with their pasts and their passions. I have sat across from them at coffee shops as they have cried and laughed. I have been in theaters, churches, and classrooms with storytellers practicing for an upcoming show and have marveled at the supportive power that arises. Individuals who were once strangers bond over their unique narratives and the courageous step they are about to take together by sharing their truths on stage. That rehearsal room is a place of magic. It is where many storytellers realize, perhaps for the first time, that few of us are as alone as we think. There is great power when someone steps on stage in front of a room full of people to claim their story as their own, but just as in any great narrative, the climax is only as powerful as the journey.

As you read through this book, please keep in mind that these stories were transcribed from live performances. They have been edited for the page, but we strove to maintain each storyteller's authentic voice. You can listen to the live audio of each story by scanning the QR codes throughout.

I want to thank each of the storytellers featured in this book, and ALL of the storytellers over the past four years who have embarked on the journey of discovering and sharing their stories. It is a courageous thing to open your heart for others to see the scars as well as the joy. Storytellers, thank you for showing us your humanity and reminding us of our own. I hope that we can all strive to be as brave as you by telling our truths and showing each other that we might be a little more alike than we are different.

—Hilary Trudell, co-founder and executive producer of The Yarn

MOLLY REED

My mother has always asked "The Questions."

They always have a capital Q, and they are always asked with the injured, fearful air of somebody who has been considering *all* of the possible answers for a very long time.

When I was twelve, I smashed my finger between my home's old-school glass water jug and its ceramic stand. Because I lived a sheltered life that had known no pain, I passed out. I woke to my mother shaking me anxiously. Her first question was, "Molly! Molly . . . are you anorexic?"

I answered, "No!"

She made me eat six peanut butter crackers in front of her just to make sure.

When I was fourteen, my mother shook me awake from a dead sleep. Admittedly, it was two o'clock in the afternoon. She asked me, "Molly, are you depressed?"

With supreme teenage annoyance, I blearily answered, "No. I just stayed up late reading. *God*."

She threw open the curtains, drew up the blinds, and refused to leave my room until I promised I would get up, take a shower, and go outside to look at the sky.

When I was seventeen, I ordered fried chicken, waffles, and a chocolate milkshake at IHOP. She stared at me for a long moment before she asked, "Molly, are you pregnant?"

Devoted Christian teen that I was, I almost choked on my chicken while I rushed to assure her, "No! I am *definitely* not pregnant. *Yes*, I am sure . . . well, of course, I can be sure, Mom . . . because *I'm a virgin,* okay?!"

The waitress was so embarrassed that my milkshake was free.

Four years of silence had lulled me into a false sense of security. I began to assume that all of life's big questions had been answered satisfactorily.

Forty minutes into a three-hour drive to Fayetteville, the car was quiet. Soft rolls of pine-covered mountain tops bisected with concrete and electrical lines passed by my window. I could see my breath fogging up the pane, and I leaned forward to make the patch bigger. I lifted my finger to scribble some temporary graffiti.

"Molly, are you dating Afton?" My stomach disappeared from my body. I stared at my paintbrush finger, and with a sticky, numb mouth, I tried for a casual, "What?"

My voice broke. Swallow. *Swallow*.

"Why would you ask that?"

I could hear the steering wheel creak under her hands. I watched a drop of condensation bleed toward the sill, suddenly completely fascinated with its trajectory.

"I had a dream," she told me.

A laugh huffed from my constricted diaphragm, and I turned in an agony of surprise and horror to face her—my sharp, small mother. My heart beat cold against my forehead, and time moved like molasses while I counted the freckles on her face, drifted over the scars under her eyes, noted with squeamish alarm the grays that were appearing in her dark hair.

Cindy is a woman of prescience. She is uncanny with her sharp, green gaze and the blazing protection of her righteous, ruthless curiosity. She once predicted her uncle's death the night before he died.

In college, she shamed a ghost by throwing open a shower curtain, stomping her foot, and screaming, "Are you happy now, you dirty old perv?" The creepy chuckling that had been haunting the girls' bathroom disappeared and was never heard from again.

At that moment in the car, my mother's face was an achingly familiar, beautiful blank, while she waited for me to break her heart.

I wasn't ready. I am never ready when she forces the truth from me—on me.

"A dream?" My voice sounded distant and slow in my ears.

The screws at the edges of her mouth tightened, and glass fell from her mouth, glistening, hard, broken.

"Are you dating her?" Quietly this time.

I hovered over myself, reaching an incorporeal hand to cover my own mouth as I listened with horror and heard myself answer, "Yes."

It hurt to look at her. So instead I looked out the window, the faintest trace of the line I had drawn earlier still visible. Wet tires swooshed underneath us, and we held ourselves tightly together, trying not to let the space around us touch. I almost fell asleep with the tension, I was so enthralled by it.

Her plaintive "Why?" washed over the silence and drowned it.

Mind pictures of *dance, kiss, touch, soft, love, friend* bombarded my senses. Sensual syntax that defies words—is cheapened by words—crowded my cerebellum. My doodling hand grasped my chest, and my mouth worked like it knew that words should be coming out.

"Why" is too big a question. Classic parent stumper and philosopher's friend, it asks for everything and is never satisfied. "Why" will make you crazy. I had driven myself half-mad for months with "Why"—from the moment that my lips had touched hers.

When I let it, "Why" crushed me, heavy and ecclesiastical, into the ground. It left the imprint of the carpet on my back with its weight. It stole the voices of my sister and my friends and my church, and it pinned me to the ground with them. "Why" stole my peace and my curiosity, my giddy joy in new love.

And now, it quashed my words until all I could do was stare at my mother's profile and say, "I don't know."

So many questions followed that to enumerate them all would be a false memory. I answered with gender studies textbooks and coming out pamphlets. I mentioned subcultures and the patriarchy. I quoted statistics on sexual assault and waxed rhapsodic about changing church views and the socioeconomic equality of a female pair, the understanding and kinship of an oppressed minority group.

I wove a tapestry of pleading and convincing around me like protection without it ever touching me. As the tapestry became thicker, more insulating, I started to panic. I was being backed into a corner that I wasn't ready to be in. I was being trapped by my own reasons.

I had been conditioned my whole life to answer incredibly personal, bluntly-asked questions at deeply inconvenient moments. It felt like I should know the answer. Like I should be able to grasp and relay more clearly, more eloquently, the answer to, "But *why* are you gay?"

The rest of that two-hour conversation, and all the other conversations that happened over the next five years, left me wounded. Some of those wounds were self-inflicted. Some were left by family, close friends, coworkers.

They were wounds of misunderstanding, of being labeled, compartmentalized, of raging against the idea that I was going to be defined by this one, small part of myself.

Coming out was supposed to be liberating. I found it agonizing.

I watched as all the other pieces of myself—my love of language, my empathy, my obsession with *Buffy the Vampire Slayer*, my deep and abiding hatred for broccoli—faded behind my queerness.

It took me a long time to realize that the problem was not my fumbling, confused answers. It was the question itself.

When you tell someone your name or your age, they don't ask you, "Why?"

You are named as your parents choose. Your age is based on the date of your birth. They might ask you "Why" if you tell them your favorite color is lavender or that you prefer angry girl punk to indie rock.

"Why" implies a condition of choice. It suggests that there is a whole other way of being. And your way is just plain *wrong*.

Eight years later, hindsight has granted me the wisdom that I lacked at twenty-one. Now, when I come out—which, as many of you in this room know, is a *daily* event—I smile serenely into the face of every sneering "Why," and I respond with the word that never asks for anything in return and is always satisfied. The word with which I wish I had answered my mother all of those years ago . . .

Love.

Listen to Molly Tell Her Story Live:

MEOSHA "YOSH" HOWARD

I first acknowledged that I was a little curious and confused about my sexuality when I was thirteen or fourteen years old. One of my friends was hanging out at the house. She looked over and was like, "Can I have some sugar?" I paused for a second, and I'm like, "That may be a little gay, but why not?" thinking about old movies where the best friends practice kissing or whatever. After I said that, she looked at me, confused. She was like, "No, I literally just wanted a spoonful of sugar." So we just sat there for a second in an awkward silence, and we never mentioned anything else about it.

At fifteen or sixteen, I started hanging out with one of the girls on the basketball team. We became good friends. One day, she wrote to me on Facebook and was like, "Meosha, I want to tell you something, but I don't want you to not be my friend anymore." I'm like, "Okay, cool." So she tells me, "Meosha, I'm gay." And me being a little ignorant, I didn't really know the extent of what that meant. She said, "Well, I'm attracted to women, and I don't date men." Because we were friends, I felt comfortable enough confiding in her about my own confusion and curiosities and my feelings and attraction towards women as well.

One night, we were supposed to go to a party, but because I'm the only girl, and I have three brothers, my parents really weren't comfortable with me going out to a party by myself. So instead, we ended up grabbing some pizza and a movie and coming back to my house. We were hanging out, having a good time, and everybody went to sleep. One thing led to another, and we explored those things that I had been so curious about for such a long time. I just remember feeling alive and feeling an awakening within me. I felt free in that moment.

Just my luck, the next day, we take a random family trip. It's me, my siblings, and my mom in the car. I just remember feeling heavy and ashamed, feeling guilt, like what I did was not normal and wasn't okay. And honestly, that feeling was something that resonated in me for the next long years of my life.

With that feeling, I didn't really want to acknowledge that part of myself.

I'm so sorry. Give me a second.

I didn't want to acknowledge that part of myself, so we really had an on-and-off-again situation for the next twelve years. I can honestly say that she was the first person that I fell in love with, but I could never commit to her the way that I wanted to because I was not comfortable being in love with another woman. It was just something that I couldn't accept about myself.

Within those twelve years, I did date men, and I am attracted to men, but my attraction to women was just always something within me that I wanted to explore but felt guilty about. I felt like it wasn't okay for me to do that until I just got frustrated.

Randomly, one day, I was scrolling on Instagram, and I came across an old crush from high school. I don't know what it was about her, maybe her eyes or her smile, but it just ignited something within me. So like a millennial would, I slid into her DMs. Who would have imagined that by me doing that, I would have fallen in love? The struggle went away because I started acknowledging that I wasn't in love with a woman. I was in love with a person. I was in love. And you know, when you fall in love, you just want to shout it from the mountaintops. Somebody loved me, and I loved them back.

It just so happened that she lived out of state, so I would go and visit her. I felt that free and alive feeling again, being able to hold hands with her out in public and showing PDA. She took me to Lesbian Happy Hour. It was like a dream. It was an oasis of beautiful lesbian, queer, femme women having a good time. They were all free. It normalized my feelings.

But when I would come back home, I would feel that heaviness all over again. It was like, *Why can't I feel like that here*? And so, one day, I'm telling my coworker about this spot that I went to, and she's like, "Meosha, you should do that here." And I'm like, "Yeah, we should have that." But then again, how the hell am I going to do that, and I'm not out? I'm not open with myself yet.

I finally got the gumption. It took me an entire year to hit publish on Little Rock Queer Girls Night Out. I remember our first meetup. We were going to call it Hello Kitty Saturdays. I sat in the car for an entire thirty minutes, if not more, just sweating and nervous. Not because I was going into a bar by myself, but because I knew that by walking through those doors, I was acknowledging a part of me that I had struggled for so long with accepting. When I finally walked through those doors, I felt that alive and that free feeling again, and it was even better because it was at home. I was being honest and transparent with myself and being honest and transparent with other people.

The group has done so many things for me. It's been extremely therapeutic, because it's amazing being able to meet other women who understand those struggles that I went through. We can laugh, and we can cry. We can talk about feeling that guilt and breaking through. It greatly exceeded my expectations.

A lot of people would ask, "Why would you come out in such a public way?" If I could save the next person twelve years of an internal struggle, the turmoil, the guilt—the unnecessary guilt—I would do it again and again and again in a heartbeat. Because who would have thought in a million years that the girl who just wanted some sugar would be in a room full of strangers saying, "I am Yosh Howard, and I am pansexual."

Listen to Yosh Tell Her Story Live:

SPENCER LUCKER

My name is Spencer Lucker, and I am the proud son of two gay women.

That line hasn't always been the easiest to say. In fact, it took sixteen years for me to first say that or some form of it to my closest friends, twenty-one years to share it with casual acquaintances, and twenty-six years to say it publicly in a social setting. That was not the case because of shame, but it was the case because of fear, confusion, and language.

How do I describe myself? How do I find words, phrases, and descriptions that neatly fit in our hetero-dominant society, which for so long has focused on family meaning husband and wife with child? That wasn't my experience. And yet my childhood was no different than any of you who had a mother and a father, except I had two moms. My parents did the best that they could to guide me through that confusion. From the get-go, they gave me tools. They gave me language to survive but not necessarily the language I needed to thrive in my identity.

The woman who birthed me was "my Mom." Her partner, and my other mother, was "my Meme." And over my almost thirty-one years of life, those terms, "Mom" and "Meme," have evolved with every breath that I've taken.

Both Mom and Meme played important roles in my upbringing as individuals and as a parental unit. My mom is athletic and energetic, teaching me to always try new things, appreciate nature, and explore the world around me. Meme has a cutting sense of humor, an incredibly competitive spirit, and the ability to make a story ten times cooler and better than the reality that you actually experienced. As a couple, they taught me compassion and empathy, integrity, a commitment to serving others, and most importantly, an undying love for family.

As a young child, my innocence was truly bliss when it came to this challenge of language and knowing that we might be a little different. I had no clue. If I ever had awkward moments, I definitely don't remember them, and I don't think they happened in my first nine years of life.

In fact, one night when I was around age six, Meme and I were heading to a church down the road to pick up my mom. They are both social workers, and my mom was facilitating a support group. We were walking down the church hallway, and there was a sign that said, "Lesbian Support Group This Way." To this day, I wish I had a picture of Meme's face when she saw that sign, because I can only imagine the horror she felt. But what did I do? I read it, head cocked in confusion, dramatically turned to Meme, and exclaimed, "Mom's a lesbian?!" (And of course, to her horror, I actually knew how to read the word "lesbian," a credit to their educational skills.)

With great wit, she responded, "Now, Spencer, just because she's at the meeting doesn't mean she's a lesbian. She's there providing information and support to women who need it." She wasn't lying because she never said that my mom wasn't a lesbian, but she had in fact used a play on words to divert the conversation.

In that moment, whether either of us recognized it or not, I had observed and learned from Meme how to use certain language tricks to actively skirt conversations that I wasn't comfortable handling. This was the protective shield that Meme, Mom, and now I had learned from our experiences. I imagine this is a shield that so many LGBTQ people across this world, along with their families and friends, have had to develop in order to survive.

I vividly remember the first time that I had a recognition of being a little different. In fourth grade, my teacher asked all of us in the class what we had done that weekend. Any of you who know me are not surprised that I was the first person to raise my hand and blurt out that Mom, Meme, and I had gone to the zoo.

"Is Meme your grandmother?" the teacher asked.

Confused, I very awkwardly said, "No, she's my Meme." I thought, *Stupid teacher. Like, what are you talking about?*

It seems like such a simple situation, but I was caught off-guard and immediately uncomfortable. I became cognizant that my answer was never going to be sufficient. I remember—and I can still feel it—my body tensing up, my heart racing, and my mind fogging. That was an experience and a feeling that I would get for many years to come anytime I was asked about more than just "my mom" or "my parents."

From then deep into high school, I self-corrected. I learned to always say either "my mom" or "my parents" when referencing either of them individually or collectively. It still never felt right because I had effectively removed the word "Meme"—a word that was so important to me—from my public lexicon.

It pains me to realize how many opportunities I missed out on telling people that 50% of me came from this person who is so very much a part of me, and I a part of her. She is so much more than some unspoken person that people probably assumed was my dad when I used the term, "my parents."

In college, with a growing presence of gay peers more openly moving along in our society and culture, I began to feel a little more comfortable in one-on-one situations talking about Meme and Mom as individuals and the great mothers that each of them are. Yet I still often fumbled that language and would quickly revert to, "Well, my parents this, my parents that," or just "I did this with my mom." This long-time habit was quite hard to break. I wasn't proud of it, but it was a habit I knew I had to work myself out of. I remember a fraternity brother interrupting me during a conversation I was having within a group in which I referenced my parents.

"You realize that we all know you have two moms, right?" he said. I feel so stupid now, but I was shocked. I had been embracing my "secret" because I didn't know how to talk about it.

He followed with, "Not only do we know, but I hope you recognize that we still like you, and better yet, we really like your parents. We kind of like them more than you." My friends continue to this day to say that. Beyond being a minor shot to my self-esteem, it also, I believe, was the single most important thing that I needed to hear to lift that shield and to open up my language. His bluntness brought a reality that was so refreshing and allowed me to think more openly about myself and my family.

In the '90s when I was coming of age, there were no gay families in pop culture. Hell, there weren't gay families in Little Rock, Arkansas, at all as far as I saw. I reflect on this often to remind myself how much my parents really were trailblazers of their time. They took extreme risks day after day, and I remind myself often that some of the fear and confusion I might've felt over my thirty years of life paled in comparison to what my parents experienced in the '70s when they were coming out pre-Harvey Milk, in the '80s when they were choosing to have a child pre-*Will & Grace* and all the pop culture that has made being gay kind of cool, in the '90s and '00s when they were raising me about as well as any parents possibly can pre-*Windsor* and pre-*Obergefell* before they could officially be married.

Now things are a bit different. Five and a half years ago, as a Washington, D.C. resident, I was able to go to the Supreme Court and stand proudly as an ally fighting against DOMA, the Defense of Marriage Act, and the many other rights of LGBTQ people that are infringed upon. I proudly held up two signs that read, "Proud child of two women in love for 33 years." I have since crossed it off twice more for Supreme Court decisions in 2015 and 2018 to show "36 years" and "38 years and counting." The other sign says, "Success, happiness, and love all thanks to my two moms."

Holding that sign in June 2013 was the first time that I had ever publicly expressed who my family was, who my parents were. I used the term "my moms." And you know what? It felt great. It felt natural because it was my truth.

The best feeling, though, came a few minutes later when I got a tap on the shoulder and turned around to see a young guy, probably in fourth grade or so, who asked to take his picture with me. He was holding a sign that said, "My moms are awesome." Obviously, my heart melted as I realized how awesome it is that he not only lives in a world where he has the language to express himself and express his love for his family and his moms at a young age, but that he can do it in such a public setting, so out loud to the rest of the world. I'd like to think that my parents played a role in that.

A year from when that picture was taken, I had the honor of planning my parents' wedding in Washington, D.C. As I approach thirty-one years of age, my parents approach their fifth wedding anniversary and, more importantly, their fortieth anniversary of being a couple.

Now I am able to stand here in public with the language, the confidence, and the comfort to say, "My name is Spencer Lucker, and I am the proud son of two gay women."

Listen to Spencer Tell His Story Live:

JUSTIN SARLO

I was born in Little Rock at St. Vincent Hospital in 1955. My parents already had two sons, and they were really excited to bring home what they thought was a little girl. They named me Sandy Kay. When I was eight years old, I told my parents that I was a boy. To be fair, in their defense, the year was 1963. There were Cuban missiles going, a war going, and a president being shot. Nobody had ever heard what transgender was.

Their response was kind of, "No, you're not. No, you're not a boy. You're a girl." Back then, you tried to live to respect your parents, so I tried to live the life they wanted for me. I dated boys, but as each year went by, and as puberty came on, my skin began to feel as if it were on fire because I wasn't a girl. And yet my body told me I was. To get rid of the pain, I wanted to rip my skin off.

When I was twenty-two, I stepped in front of a truck. Luckily, it missed. I discovered that if I drank enough—vodka mostly—the pain would go away for that night. I would wake up the next morning, and it would be back with a hangover, but at least for one night I could be numb.

I met a man, and we got married. He also drank. When my two sons came along, I decided perhaps I needed to learn to live with the pain because I was a mom. So I sobered up. He didn't. Eventually, we divorced. And I raised my kids as a single mom and a lesbian who wasn't really a lesbian. That was as close as I could get. I figured I had done enough damage to my kids by being those two things that I could never really be who I still really wanted to be.

Life went on. I learned to live with pain.

In April 2011, we were doing a benefit for Lucie's Place, a coalition to help LGBT homeless youth named after a young lady, Lucie, who was a transgender woman. After the benefit, I was introduced to Lucie's mom. My normal way of flirting with somebody I think is beautiful is to mumble a lot and stare at the tops of my shoes. So I was doing that, and she said to me, "So how long have you been transitioning?" I said, "Shh. Nobody knows this. I'm not, no, not, no, I'm not. No."

In May of 2011, my two sons, their wives, and I were all together for Memorial Day weekend. My son said, "Mom, we want to talk to you."

Being a lifelong smoker, I said, "I promise I'll quit smoking."

They said, "Yes, we wish you would, but that's not why we want to talk to you." My two sons, the only two people in the world who really mattered to me, wanted to tell me that if I wanted to transition, they fully supported me. I had never told anyone, but they knew.

So, I came flying out of the closet the second time, like a teenager on Facebook, posting "I'm trans." To which most of my friends and family said, "Yeah."

Fast forward a few more years to last July, and that beautiful young woman I met at the Lucie's Place benefit became my wife.

So, listen, I want to tell y'all something. At eight years old, if somebody had said to me, "Someday, you'll get to be yourself, and you'll get to be happy," I would have never believed them. Certainly at twenty-two, I wouldn't have believed them, but I have to tell y'all, today may not be okay. Tomorrow may not be either. But someday, it will be okay. And until then, if you need someone to talk to, I am here, whether you're gay, straight, Black, white, trans . . . I know what it's like to be different. I'm always here on Facebook, loud and clear. So please look me up.

Listen to Justin Tell His Story Live:

ANNA KIMMELL

I am 135 pounds, and I am a junior in college pursuing a degree in musical theatre. Despite the warnings, I have gained the "freshman fifteen" pounds, and the last few years my weight has fluctuated up and down, depending on my activity level.

As far as theatre was concerned, I didn't really feel like I was on par with my peers at this time. Everyone was very confident and excited about auditioning. I was not confident or excited about auditioning, so I didn't book a lot of work, either at school or professionally. I felt behind. But the summer after my sophomore year of college, I booked my first professional gig at a wonderful theater in North Carolina. I spent four months living and breathing theatre. I even got a couple of roles and was feeling a lot better about where I was in the industry.

The last two days of that contract, a "friend" of mine asked, "Why are you wearing those baggy clothes? Is it to hide all the weight you've gained?"

I was shocked and upset and furious, and I told him, "No, you cannot talk to me like that, and you cannot talk to anybody else like that." But he never apologized, and I wrote him off as an asshole, which he was. But I couldn't shake his words. So the fall of my junior year of college, I committed to losing some weight. It started off with me having an awareness of what I was eating. I cut bread, I didn't eat as much fat or sugar, and I was enrolled in a lot of dance classes for my major. So the weight just started falling off.

133 . . . 130 . . . 128 . . . 125

I was feeling a little bit better about how my body looked, and every pound I lost was exhilarating because

I was accomplishing a goal. So I kept going.

124 . . . 121 . . . 120

That was the weight I was when I started college, and it felt really good.

118 . . . 116 . . . 113

That's about the time when people started noticing, and they said, "Wow, you look amazing, how are you doing this?" And I would answer, "Portion control," which was true-ish. By that point, it had become more of an obsession than anything else. I was eating between 800 and 1,000 calories a day while the recommended calorie intake for somebody my size is 1,500, and I was dancing between two and four hours a day pretty rigorously. So I was easily burning off everything I consumed.

I remember being in a second or third costume fitting, the designer pulling at the extra fabric. He turned me around, and said, "You can't lose any more weight. I can take this in one more time, but you can't lose any more weight."

112 . . . 109 . . . 107

In modern dance, you roll on the floor a lot. Well, in my class, we did just that, and I was covered in bruises—big welts on my back and my shoulders—because I had no fat on my body and no more muscle tone.

I also remember looking in the mirror in my dorm room, noticing that my thighs didn't touch anymore, and thinking, "Oh, I'll never let that happen again."

106 . . . 104 . . . 101

Around that time, I stopped stepping on the scale because I knew that I was out of control, and I couldn't stop it. What's really unfortunate is that I started booking a lot of work. I started getting the roles that I had wanted. I booked a summer in Colorado, and I booked Audrey in *Little Shop*, and Rapunzel in *Into the Woods,* and it was of course, to me, related to my weight loss. My success was because of my weight loss.

I probably got down to about 99 pounds. I was feeling dizzy all the time, on the verge of passing out at any given moment. I was very sick. I was starving.

After rehearsal one day, a teacher who I very much admired, a choreographer, grabbed my bicep here, which was about the size of my wrist now, and said, "This has to stop." And it wasn't warm, and it wasn't gentle, but it was effective.

I would love to tell you all right now that was the moment when everything got better. I gained some weight back, and I sought help, but that's not true. I struggled with anorexia for the next eight years. In my mind, I thought I looked really good at about 103 pounds.

Now, I finally have this bird's eye perspective of the experience, and I see these flashbulb memories in my childhood and adolescence that show that I was somewhat predisposed to this. I remember being seven, so tiny, and in a dance class, and noticing that my belly was hanging out, and quickly sucking it in and thinking, "Ew, that's gross." I remember Grandma saying, "Don't get any more dessert." And then in college, being surrounded by a group of people who were obsessed with how they looked and what they weighed and having that language swirling around me. "Oh, I have a big audition, and I have to lose that weight," or "I'm fasting before opening so I can fit into my costume." It's infectious, and it's really hard to rise above that when you're in it.

Now, I am a dance and theatre teacher, and I talk to students ages five to eighty about how their bodies are instruments for expression. Of course, if people want to pursue theatre or dance professionally, your body type is part of the industry, but I'm very, very cautious about how I talk about type. I want my students to feel empowered and celebrate what their bodies can do, not obsess over what they look like.

I'll leave you all with some lyrics from one of my favorite musical theatre composers, Stephen Sondheim. This is a lyric from *Into the Woods*, and it's a reminder that your language can shape someone else's reality, for better or for worse.

"Careful the things you say, children will listen. Careful the things you do. Children will see and learn."

Listen to Anna Tell Her Story Live:

LORENZO LEWIS

It was a cold, winter day in December of 1997. I was eight years old and in third grade. I can remember the sound of the telephone ringing in the early morning hours. I woke up in a cold sweat because my heart was beating. After the telephone stopped ringing, I heard an echo on the other end. Chaos. My auntie, who answered the telephone, screamed hysterically and shouted, "Your father has passed." I was confused and disoriented as if my heart was twisting—nauseous to the stomach.

As a little boy who barely knew his father, I began to ask myself, *Where do I go from here? What is next? How will my life be now that he is gone?*

At school, I experienced various issues socializing with peers, tearing up the classroom, and giving the teachers a very hard time. I was struggling from grief, and my family was non-responsive, as I come from a cultural group who believes to pray and only to pray. This was hard, and it got so hard that recommendations were made. In order for me to stay in school, I had to go and spend eight weeks at a facility camp for boys and girls to work on my emotional issues.

There was a very long ride, and it felt really gloomy as the rain poured. I can remember feeling very lost. The tears dropped from my eyes as if crocodile tears were coming. I could feel the tears fall on my feet as if they came from a bucket of water. I felt really hurt to know that I would spend eight weeks away from home with only weekend passes.

How would I live in this place?

I began to sit into a comfort of knowing that I had reached a safe place. The people were very nice and generous, and my camp counselor, Mr. Jesse, became a very dear friend. We learned archery. We learned how to roast marshmallows. We hiked. We hunted. We learned how to do mock trials as if we were politicians. It taught us leadership and civic engagement. This was very inspirational, and to go through these different things was great.

Fast forward thirteen years later. I'm twenty-one years old at the University of Arkansas at Pine Bluff. I'm a sophomore at the time. Life is great. And as a sophomore in college, it is all about partying. Sleepless nights and having a really, really good time. I felt that I was at the peak of my life. Well, that same phone call resurrected again, but this time I answered the telephone, and, ladies and gentlemen, on the other side of the telephone would be a life-altering experience. I can hear, again, the deep, hysterical scream, but this time it was my sister. Our mother has passed.

At twenty-one years old, I sit on the side of my bed, feet dangling, asking myself, *Is this just a dream? Can this be true? Surely this is not happening. I am now twenty-one years old with merely a relationship with my biological mother and father, and they're both gone.* My heart felt ripped, and I could really feel the emotion and the drain.

I did my best by staying in school that semester. I had some failing grades. I can remember not talking to others, being very withdrawn, continuously thinking about her in the casket and how I really felt, continuously having those conversations with myself. *If only I had gotten to know her a little bit better.*

I was experiencing depression, and it was undiagnosed. As I continue to move forward, it is part of my life.

I took a semester off from school, my grades were so poor. I said, *Well, hey, I could just work*. So, I started to look for a job.

Someone approached me and said, "Hey, you're a big fellow. Hey, won't you come and work for the juvenile?" I began to think, *This is very odd for me to want to work in such a horrific place.* But I had to also ask myself, *Someone would possibly be there for me, why don't I be there for someone else?*

As I worked at this place, I was inspired. I began to increase the engagement with the youth and cultivate the lives of the young beings that I had permission to work with. It was a life-changing event. I spent nine years working in Behavioral Health at Rivendell, Bridgeway, and other places in Central Arkansas. I was privileged to work in this space and to be able to work with others.

But something was not quite right. I noticed I was seeing myself sometimes through the patients. I began to have flashbacks of me being eight years old. At times I would even shut down. I noticed males that looked just like myself, that wouldn't buy into the treatment. I wondered why. I began to do my synopsis and ask questions of why guys that look like myself can't submit themselves or open up freely.

As I did this, I began to pray and ask for a vision of how I could help with this change. I had a vision to create The Confess Project. I noticed a stigma between African American males and how hard it is to be masculine and to be open. I noticed that the stigma is very strong and that I struggled with the same issues. As I began to develop this vision of The Confess Project, I wanted it to be a model built for boys and men of color to be expressive and be held in safe spaces.

I create safe spaces. What are safe spaces? We create programming, monthly empowering sessions. We create initiatives where I go into the barbershop and hold healthy dialogues with gentlemen about emotional and mental health. I was inspired to do that because my story is a vessel for wanting to change the narrative. I knew that my story could change the narrative if I could just have a chance. The Confess Project is my chance.

I'll leave you with this: I've reached men that are shattered and broken.

I've reached men that are lost and weary.

I've reached men to let them know that we all have a purpose.

Usually I find that they're right there, reaching back.

Listen to Lorenzo Tell His Story Live:

RICK OWEN

When I started medical school at the University of Minnesota, I had no idea that I would become a psychiatrist. But I was fascinated as I learned about the brain and the frontiers of neuroscience, and when I first talked to patients with mental illnesses, I was hooked. I enjoyed listening to their life stories and trying to understand what was going on with them and how to help them. At the time I chose psychiatry as a career, I had not had any symptoms of mental illness.

I moved to Boston after medical school, starting my medical internship by working nights in the emergency room of a community hospital. After a few weeks of switching between day and night shifts, I couldn't sleep. I started feeling stressed out all the time. Nothing could make me smile.

The next month, I started working on the internal medicine ward. Working might be too strong a word because my brain had stopped functioning. I couldn't concentrate or make simple decisions. I didn't feel sad or depressed—it was more like I was in a state of shock. Feeling like a failure at my intended career. Feeling desperate. Feeling afraid that I might kill a patient.

Within a week, I told my supervisor, "I want to quit." He said, "Rick, you're depressed." He arranged for me to see a psychiatrist later that day. But I thought what I had wasn't something that could be treated or cured. I went home before going to see the psychiatrist, and it just sort of hit me. I was quitting my job. My life was ruined. The ground was cracking and falling away beneath my feet. I found a bottle of paint thinner and thought about drinking it to kill myself, but then I read the warning label (DANGER ☠ POISON . . . MAY BE FATAL OR CAUSE BLINDNESS IF SWALLOWED). It would probably just make me really sick, or blind me, but not end my life.

Then I got out a butcher knife and held it to my chest with the point over my heart. I started to press. But I'm risk-averse, and I'm squeamish. In a strange way, I was lucky that I was so depressed. In my clouded thinking, I knew I would fail at anything I attempted. And since I believed I had just quit my job, I would have no health insurance to pay for treatment after my failed suicide attempt, and then I'd be an even bigger failure.

Somehow, I made it to the psychiatrist's office. After a few questions, he said, "Rick, you're depressed." Then he asked, almost as an afterthought, "You're not having any thoughts of suicide, are you?" I said, "Well, maybe a little." I did not want to tell this man who would later become a mentor and colleague how bad off I was. I was too ashamed to tell him what was going on in my head. You're not supposed to talk about these things! He gave me a prescription for an antidepressant and sent me home.

My family wanted to help, and their idea was that my dad, a physician, would fly out from Minneapolis and talk me into continuing my internship. When he saw me, he realized I needed far more help than he could provide. Plan B was to take me back to Minneapolis to meet with my medical school advisor, a psychiatrist, so that he could talk some sense into me.

Over the next day, waiting to fly back to Minneapolis with my dad, my thoughts became more and more bizarre. I believed I had killed a patient and that the police were after me as a result. When we arrived at the airport the next evening, I thought the police were supposed to come and arrest me, to prevent me from getting on the plane.

But we got on the plane and the plane took off. I'm not sure why, but I became convinced the plane was going to crash. I kept saying that to my father sitting next to me, poor guy. By the time we landed in Minneapolis, it was like the world had come apart. I thought there had been a nuclear war and believed I was the cause of it.

The next morning, we went to see my former medical school advisor. After a brief chat, he walked me down the hall to the locked psychiatric unit. I spent two and a half months there, most of it accompanied by a sitter on suicide watch. They gave me some medications that caused more side effects than benefit. Finally, they offered me electroconvulsive therapy, sometimes known as "shock therapy." For many, this term reminds them of the gruesome scene in the film, *One Flew Over the Cuckoo's Nest*, but ECT is safe these days and administered in a humane manner. I told my doctors that I was ready to try anything that might help.

After the first treatment, I knew it was going to work. My mood lifted a bit, I felt more energetic and I began to have hope about the future. After six more treatments, I was doing well, and was soon discharged from the hospital. At that point, all I wanted to do was get back to Boston and resume my medical internship and psychiatry training. While I was welcomed back by my fellow trainees and supervisors after my return, I did not get the same collegial response from the Massachusetts Medical Licensing Board. When I filled out my license renewal, there was a question, "Have you been treated for a mental illness?" I indicated that I had and filled in additional details as requested, including my hospitalization and treatment for depression.

As a result, I had to meet with the licensing board director, who seemed very concerned about my illness. He said I would have to get a letter from a psychiatrist every month saying that I was fit to practice medicine. I didn't like that, but I agreed, because I just wanted to continue my training, so I agreed.

The next year, I had to renew my license, encountering the same question on the renewal form and giving the same answer. This time they called me into a meeting of the full licensing board. After waiting for hours, I was called up to the table at the front of the room.

The chair of the board, an attorney, said to me, "Dr. Owen, if you had had the flu instead of major depression, would you be here today?" I said no, and my license was granted with no more supervision required.

So that's a happy ending to the story. Right? But for a long time, I was afraid to talk about my illness—afraid to tell anyone what I had been through. After more than ten years had passed, I started telling my closest friends about my experiences. I became more comfortable talking about my illness, even in public, after I joined the board of directors of the National Alliance on Mental Illness (NAMI) Arkansas, whose mission is to provide support, education, and advocacy for those living with a mental illness, their families, and friends. Being active in that organization meant that telling my story was expected and welcomed.

I've been very lucky in my life. Although I have bipolar disorder, I have had excellent health care, insurance to pay for that care, and a supportive family. I am a mental health advocate because I believe that getting good mental health care should not be a matter of luck. I want every individual with a mental illness to be able to get help promptly, to get quality health care, and to not be harmed by stigma or discrimination. I've learned in my life that telling my story lets other people know that there is help and hope.

Listen to Rick Tell His Story Live:

DAVID FISCHMAN

It was the end of the first year of medical school, and I felt like a badass. I was doing pretty well in school, I was going to be the first doctor in my family, I was still beefy from playing rugby, I was climbing a lot, and I was pretty impressed with myself.

I was climbing with a big group of friends, a bunch of them in medical school with me, and they had just built this amazing new gym in Albuquerque with gigantic fifty-foot walls. I was climbing often, particularly with my buddy Stephen. He was a couple of years ahead of me and a fantastic climber.

Stephen and I were at the gym, at the end of a pretty brutal climbing session of about an hour and a half, two hours. Stephen wanted to go on one more route. If you are the lead climber, you wear a harness to which the rope is tied. You climb, or scamper up the wall if you're feeling good, and clip the rope into a clip. Then, the rope runs from your harness to the little clip on the wall and back down to the belayer, through their belay device, and into their hand. All you've got to do as the belayer is keep your hand on that rope, pull down on the rope, and your climber is not going to fall. It's pretty simple.

So, Stephen scampers up the wall. This guy's in his element. I'm belaying. It's crowded, easily one hundred people in the gym. My other buddy, Mike, is next to me. He's been out of town for a while, so we are getting caught up. Stephen is making good progress, just hauling ass up this wall as Mike and I are talking. All of a sudden Mike's eyes jump. He yells, "Dave!" and points at my harness. I look down. The rope isn't in my hands and is absolutely flying through the belayer device.

I look up, and Stephen is plummeting towards me. Just a moment ago he was all the way at the top of the wall fifty feet up. Now I have to make a decision to step out of the way, and let him fall, because I know he's going to hit the ground. I can't grab that rope. It looks like a lightning bolt, whipping all over the place as the slack runs out. Desperately, I squeeze the rope between my forearm and my chest, trying to slow it down.

He hits.

For a moment there's dead silence in the gym. Then, blood sputters out of Stephen's mouth. He makes this horrible sound, like a moan, and cries. People start screaming. They swarm him. I just stand there.

I let him fall. He was just at the top of the wall. All I had to do was keep my fucking hand on the rope. That's it, and I didn't. And now he's on the ground, and he's dying, or he's maimed forever.

The paramedics come. They rush him to the hospital. My friends help him get out of the harness. I can't even untie the rope. I'm losing my fucking mind. I run to my car, shut the door. I turn the ignition. I race off to the hospital, freaking out the entire way, just screaming at myself. My voice is hoarse. I can taste blood at the back of my throat by the time I get to the hospital.

I wait, and I wait, just watching his terrified parents sit across the room, waiting for news on how Stephen is doing. I wait for ages. Finally, someone comes out. Stephen's okay. He has three broken bones in his back, but he's going to be okay. He has a horrible concussion but no life threatening injuries. Relief washes over me.

I go back to see him. He's in this big resuscitation bay, about half the size of this room. Inside that bay is a little ring of curtains, and inside that ring is a little bed. On that bed is Stephen. I step inside the ring.

He looks up at me and goes, "Dave, man, I got really hurt. But I think I'm going to be okay. Wow. I don't remember anything."

"Well, Steve, you were climbing. I was belaying. You passed the top, and then something happened. You hopped off. I don't know. I wasn't paying attention, and I dropped you. You hit the ground. I'm so sorry."

"Oh, Dave, that's terrible. I'm so sorry. Are you okay? You must feel terrible. Don't beat yourself up. Mistakes happen." Then he'd talk some more, and then he'd stop and get this weird look in his face. Then he'd look at me and repeat, "Don't beat yourself up, man. It looks like I'm going to be okay. Wow."

I'd tell him again, "Stephen, I dropped you. It's my fault. I'm sorry." Without hesitation, again, he'd say, "Oh my God, I'm sorry. Are you okay? You must feel terrible. Don't beat yourself up. Mistakes happen." Again with this look on his face. And then he said, "Dave . . ."

He was stuck on repeat. Every five minutes, without hesitation, he'd look at me, and he would forgive me immediately. This mistake that I made had highlighted all of my worst qualities. I was reckless, vain, over-confident. I didn't want to forgive myself. I felt like forgiving myself was giving myself permission to continue being this person. Considering what I want to do with my life—be a physician, save lives, make important decisions—I needed to do a lot more than keep my hand on the fucking rope.

Continuing climbing was some sort of way to get through whatever it was that I was going through. So, I went back to the gym, got back on the wall, climbed. I was terrified. Every time on the wall, I would see Stephen plummeting in my head. Over and over, he would fall. I'd go to the grocery store, I'd see him fall. I'd pump gas, I'd see him fall. I'd go to sleep, I'd see him fall. But I kept going. I was so scared every time in the gym, but it got a little better, over and over, and after a while, I didn't get over it, but I got through it. I didn't discard it, but it became a part of me.

The silver lining is that Stephen still climbs to this day. He has a little lingering back pain from time to time but went on to become an intensive care physician on the East Coast and is, by all accounts, totally okay now.

I went on to become an emergency medicine physician. I go in to work every day and often make life or death decisions. My job requires that I maintain a pretty high level of focus throughout a hectic shift, and dropping Stephen reminds me that focus requires mindfulness and constant effort and that I should never take it for granted. Although I still think about his fall, certainly less frequently than before, I'm grateful for this reminder of the consequences of losing focus. It's not exactly a happy ending, but it's enough.

Listen to David Tell His Story Live:

RHONNA-ROSE AKAMA-MAKIA

Africans don't fail.

It's true. I'm not quite sure if it's because of some meeting that the elders had or some twisted African version of *What to Expect When You're Expecting*, but the expectations are there. You don't fail. If by chance you do, you end up becoming a disappointment for your friends, your family, your parents, and really your entire community.

Death does something to a community built on perfection. Because in order for a community to be perfect, everyone has to play a role. And not just play that role, but be good at it. So when someone leaves, or, excuse me, when someone dies, it creates a gap, a hole. And someone else has to fill it.

When I was eleven years old, my mother died of colon cancer. With her death came a gap. A hole. A role that had to be filled. So, I filled it. I became a mother to my six-year-old sister, my one-year-old brother. I became an emotional support to a lot of adults in my life. My own childhood wasn't really considered.

My mother was amazing. She was a wife, a mother, and a sister, and she had the only profession that Africans really respect. She was a doctor. She died at age thirty-nine, so her death shook us all.

When I was twenty-one, I landed my dream job, and I was good at it. It was a perfect mixture of personal passion and being able to do good in the world. I didn't quite understand that being good at my job took everything that I had. I gave hours, weeks, months, years to further the mission that I was so attached to. I gave so much that there really wasn't a line between my job and my life.

One day, I was sitting across the dining room table from my new husband with bloodshot eyes and tears streaming down my face. He looked at me and said, "You can't do this. This is literally killing you."

So, I didn't quite understand, as I walked into the office to give my resignation letter, why I felt failure, guilt, and disappointment. There was a sense, like, *My friends, my family, my parents, my community. They are going to know*. There was a deeper hole in me.

I decided to go on a voyage to find out why this was. Like a true millennial, I began online. I looked up every hashtag I could find. I created my own. #rhonnasinnerpeace, #strawberriesontheporch. I was going to crowdsource my stability.

I did what Pinterest told me to do: I took a bath. And it was an amazing bath. I drew up warm water, put candles all around the tub, played music. I put in a bath bomb. As I got in, that warm water surrounding me, I closed my eyes and prayed for the stress to leave me. But as the water got cold and India Arie turned into Fetty Wap, I was confused. Where was my peace? Where was my comfort? Where were my answers? Only in that moment did I realize this was going to take some actual work.

I actively sought out friends, family, and others in the community that would hold me accountable and be my support system, only to find out that they'd been there the entire time, waiting on me to recognize the work that needed to be done. I went to therapy, so as not to put the burden of my healing on them by seeking professional help. I changed jobs. I ensured that my surroundings were about my actual care, not just for social media.

This deep healing took a level of bravery that I didn't really know I was capable of for a long time because I had been completely terrified of prioritizing my own mental health since so much of my life was tied to the care of others. In actively seeking out real healing, I realized I'm not perfect, but that's okay. 'Cause even though I'm not perfect, at least now I'm brave.

Listen to Rhonna-Rose Tell Her Story Live:

KEVIN HUNT, SR.

When I was in fourth, fifth, and sixth grades, I would sit in the back. I'd kick the table, fight my friends, and occasionally throw stuff at my teacher. It wasn't that I didn't like school. I was just upset and mad at my situation at home.

The difference between me and some of my friends was that when I left in the morning to go to school, I knew there was a good chance that when I got home I wouldn't see my mother. So, I was mad about that. I also knew, when I got home, that there was a good chance that our water would be cut off. So, I was mad about that. And, I knew there was a good chance that our gas would be cut off because it had been before. So, I was mad about that. And, I was mad about going to school with old, dirty, holey clothes.

I took all that anger out on my teacher.

Every time I got kicked out of class, every time I sat in the hallway, I missed out on learning. I missed learning my ABCs. I missed out on how to count from one to one hundred. I missed out on 1+1 and 2+2. I missed out on all of those things because I was so angry at my situation at home that when I got to school, I took it out on everyone that I could. I lost a lot of fights. I lost a lot period, sitting in that hallway, mad.

But I loved school. I remember the times when those lunch meals were amazing to me because I ate so many real cheese sandwiches. So many sugar sandwiches. At home, we ate bread and hot dogs or anything cheap that we could afford. We had to go next door and borrow hot water.

I probably should have been retained to the sixth grade because my learning had stopped in the fourth. But I was a basketball player. And in the eighth grade, they were waiting for me to play basketball. They didn't care that I couldn't read. They didn't care that I didn't know 5x5 or 4x4 or 2+2.

My mother was incarcerated, and I stayed with my grandmother. She already had some of my auntie's kids and all the kids in the same house with my great-grandmother. My place of peace was on that basketball court, but when I got home, all I could think of was my mother. At my grandmother's, we had a little more food, but I didn't have my mother. Halfway through my eighth grade year, my mother got home.

After eighth grade, I still couldn't read or do math. I was saying to myself, *I can't do this anymore*. Dare I go into the next grade and have the teacher call on me and tell me to read out of the textbook when I know I can't read? Telling me, "Kevin, come up to the board and do the next division problem," when I know I can't do it? I said, *No, I can't do that*.

So, the summer after my eighth grade year, I decided I was just going to drop out of school. And my friends who were going through some similar situations decided to drop out of school. I left my neighborhood in East End Little Rock and walked all the way downtown to get the coins in the fountain because fifty and seventy-five cents was a lot of money, and we used to love Now & Laters and penny candy. We used to walk down there all the time.

What I didn't know was that the path that we used to take to get those coins, right in front of the old Arkansas State House, would be the same trail where we'd start snatching purses at age thirteen or fourteen. One day, we started snatching purses, and we kept snatching purses.

Since I was already out of school, I started doing small crimes, and by the time I was fourteen or fifteen years old, I had already joined the neighborhood gang.

From gang crimes, one day I caught a felony. So, here I am fifteen, sixteen years old, my mother incarcerated again, and I can't read, write, or spell, and now I have a felony. I went before the judge, the first time I'd ever been caught by the police, and he sent me to prison. Sixteen years old, down there with a whole bunch of grown men, I was lost and confused. I did my time. Eventually, I was free and out in the world. But I can't read. I can't write. So what should I do? I went back to the same thing I had always done, over and over again.

My grandmother used to say, "Kevin, go back to school." I'd look at her and say, "Yeah, Grandma, I'm going to go back," but in my heart, I knew I wasn't going to go back because I was already defeated. For seven years I told her this, but I never went back to school. I knew I couldn't read, write, or spell, but I couldn't tell my grandmother that. I couldn't say, "Grandmother, I can't read, and I'm sixteen."

One day, I got a call from my sister who said, "Kevin, you need to go to the hospital. Your grandmother is dying." I went and talked to my grandmother, and she said she was ready to go home. For the first time in my life, I cried. She said she loved me, she loved all her grandkids, all her kids. She said I was her favorite. So I double cried.

Because of my grandmother's death, because of the lie that I always told her, because of the promise that I knew I was never going to keep, I went and signed up for Arkansas Adult Education.

When I got there, there were people that loved on me and kept loving on me and made me believe that I could read, even though I knew I couldn't read or write. They made me believe, broke down that doubt in me, put hope in me. They kept loving on me and kept loving on me.

The next thing I knew, I was able to read. The next thing I knew, I was able to write my first sentence. The next thing I knew, I was able to think better. I started planning for something past my GED. I took my GED test one time, and I passed it. Then it occurred to me to go to college. I signed up at Philander Smith College and took all the classes. I hung around all the positive people who wanted something out of life. Then I graduated. Next I went on to my master's program at university, kept learning and kept working, and finished my master's degree.

I got a job working on this campaign where this guy was running for governor. He won. People said, "Kevin, you want the job," and I'd say, "I can't work there. I've been to prison." They said, "Come interview on Sunday." I interviewed and got the job.

Now here I am—same person who couldn't read, write, or spell, mother incarcerated—working at the State Capitol in the Governor's Office. I worked there for a long time, and in my mind, they must not have gotten the memo. They didn't tell the right people that I'm not supposed to be there. The whole time in my mind, I knew one day someone was going to knock on my door and say, "Kevin, we need to have a talk." I knew, the whole time, that someone was going to call me into the office.

And one day, someone actually knocked on my door and said, "Kevin, meet us in ten minutes." That ten minutes made me think about everything I did in my life, over and over. That ten minutes made me think, *I knew this day was going to come*. As I walked from my office to their office, with every step that I took, I thought about all the things I did in my life. Every step that I took, I was thinking about how they were going to say, "Thank you for this opportunity, Kevin, but blah blah . . ."

When I got to the office, my thoughts were shrouded with negative things. They were looking at me, and I was looking at them, and they were talking, and I couldn't hear what they were saying.

Until they said, "Kevin, what do you think of this promotion?"

"What promotion?"

"The one that we just gave you."

Listen to Kevin Tell His Story Live:

MARCK BEGGS

Hello. My name is Marck, and I'm an alcoholic with neighbors. A recovering alcoholic with neighbors.

It wasn't always that way. We used to live out in the country, on a tree farm. We had three hundred acres with a private lake and a five-thousand-square-foot house with a Swedish sauna. It was paradise. The nearest neighbor was half a mile away. The only thing we ever talked about was tractors.

After fifteen years of sobriety, I started relapsing, and it was great for me because I had so much solitude and secrecy out there. But it wasn't so great for my wife. Carly was born prematurely. As a result, she's legally blind and suffers from a lot of anxiety. She can't drive. So living out there, in what most people would call paradise, was a prison to her. But we did get married out there. It's where I wrote our wedding song.

When you were born, the doctor looked into your mother's eyes,
he must have seen you then.
Too early for this world, no bigger than a baby squirrel,
your life could fall like wind.
One story can't hold a life, but it brought you here.
There's no glory being alive if we don't face the fear.

Fear is stagnation. So we faced the fear. We decided to make a change and move to Little Rock. Specifically, we moved into the People's Republic of Hillcrest.

For Carly, the results were immediate. She got the independence that she'd been craving and needed for so long. Suddenly, she could walk to the grocery store, to a coffee shop, to the gym where she works out. She could take Ubers to her part-time job at the Esse Purse Museum.

Meanwhile, I started bottoming out. If you've ever been to a twelve-step meeting, if you've ever listened to a drunkalogue, one thing that the stories all have in common is that they are very, very sad. That's not important. The real story is how you crawl out from under that rock and start to see the world the way it really is.

Our first big adjustment in Hillcrest was the fact that we had neighbors. Right outside the window, walking around. Carly had to start wearing clothes. She may be blind, but she's a free spirit. I had to turn down my guitar. Our dogs—Penny Lane, Benny Jett, and Eleanor Rigby—had to learn that they were not unique. They were not the only dogs in the universe. Hillcrest is a Eukanuba dog show in the waiting. There are fancy dogs who wear bow ties and neckerchiefs and argyle sweaters. There are funny dogs. A couple of doors down, there's one named Shadow. You see him, and he's just squirming. He wants to sit in your lap, but he's the size of a small bear, and it's just not going to happen. His owner always says, "Oh, he's big-boned."

One of the side effects of sobriety is an inclination towards self-improvement. I noticed around my neighborhood that basic house maintenance was a mystery to a lot of people. I don't know why, but the thought of bursting pipes keeps me up at night. So, when winter came, I went to the hardware store and stocked up on faucet covers. I went around at night and started putting them on my neighbors' faucets. I also noticed, as I was taking their hoses off, that a lot of them were dripping. I'd look inside and they had broken gaskets. So for the following couple of weeks, I'd be fixing those as well. When I was a kid, my uncle told me that these things are called nipples. That's my uncle for you. And so every once in a while, Carly will hear me say, "Hey, babe, I'm leaving. I'll be back. I'm going out to mount some nipples."

I also pick up trash. After waste management comes through and leaves their carnage all over the street, I pick up the trash and recycling bins and close them, particularly on rainy days.

It's not above me to pick up other people's dog poop. I always have a bag in my pocket, and I'm pretty sure I'm not the only one. I went to the hardware store once to buy one of those fake rocks that you hide a key in. And this kid there looks at me and has an epiphany. He says, "Man, they should make those things look like dog shit. And then nobody would ever touch them."

I thought for a moment, looked him in the eye, and said, "That wouldn't work in Hillcrest." Inevitably, someone would bag my key.

The other thing Carly and I had to come to terms with was the idea of fences, because out in the country we didn't have fences. When we first bought the house, it had this ugly chain link fence. So, I put in a nice big wooden fence and used part of it as an outer wall for a catio that I built. Here's the news: dogs aren't the only show in town. In Hillcrest, the cats are pretty popular too. In fact, my cat Po-poe and her catio were featured in *Hillcrest Life* magazine before they ever mentioned me and Carly at all.

In the smaller yard space, I was frustrated. I wanted to plant a garden, but with the fence and the small area, I couldn't figure anything out. One day I went to Hocott's Nursery, and this guy had taken a pallet, stood it up, and fixed up the sides. He painted it fire-engine red and put dirt and plants in it. He had turned a pallet into a vertical planter. My mind exploded. It wasn't even for sale, but in my pocket that day, I happened to have money. The pallet went home with me.

I hung it up and started researching this concept of vertical gardening. And that's where I'm at now. One of the beautiful things about sobriety is that when I look at myself in the mirror now, when I look out the window, when I walk through my neighborhood, when I see those blank spaces in my fence, I think one day I will be the king of vertical gardening in Hillcrest.

In sobriety, I found something that I almost lost to the bottle for a long time. I found neighbors and a neighborhood. I found potential. Now I see a path forward.

Listen to Marck Tell His Story Live:

JENNIFER COBB

It was 1983, the summer before seventh grade, and the last summer I remember being a child. I was twelve, not yet a teenager, but still too big to think I was a kid.

I grew up in the Heights neighborhood of Little Rock, on North Pierce Street. My brother, my best friend Suzanne—who lived across the street—and I were part of a pack of about eight kids that lived on the same block. And from the time we were little, we were that pack. Every summer, we hit front yards, back yards, and neighborhood streets when the sun came up and played until the sun went down.

At first, the games were easy. We played tag, hide and seek, red rover. As we grew up, they became a little bit more adventurous and dangerous—at least for me! There was the "dare-Jennifer-to-climb-to-the-top-of-the-swing-set-and-jump" game. There was the "stand-on-the-porch-railing-and-jump-over-the-azaleas" game. When I got my second set of stitches, my mother said, "Jennifer, Suzanne, stop. Go find another way to amuse yourselves."

So, we formed a spy club.

We had just read *Harriet the Spy*, a book about a girl who roams her neighborhood streets, writing down everything she sees in her black spy notebook. So, that's what we did.

Every good spy needs a spy route. It must be subversive and secret and dangerous. So, we started in my side yard and then ventured into my neighbor's driveway. We jumped a small retaining wall, and we scooted down the side of his house and behind his woodpile.

Our first stop on the spy route was the fence that guarded my neighbor's swimming pool. We peeked through to see who we could see. We would stare longingly at the cool water, wishing we could jump in to rinse off the hundred-degree heat.

Not finding anything interesting there, we would turn around to face a low rock wall. There was a gate in the wall, but it was a wall, and we were twelve, so of course we climbed the wall. Once we jumped over, we would land in the green easement behind the houses and walk down to the street. We were literally right around the corner from my own house, but we felt like we had come miles.

The next stop on the spy route was to hop up on my neighbor's front porch and peek in his windows. Yes, highly illegal and technically trespassing. That's what we were doing one day when we heard this raspy female voice holler, "Girls, what are you doing?"

We turned around, startled, and saw this woman standing across the street. She had on bright-colored pedal pushers and navy-blue Keds. She had fabulous salt and pepper hair wrapped in a floral scarf and wore Jackie O sunglasses and big earrings. She was standing there with one arm crossed over her chest and one arm raised in order to puff dramatically on the lit cigarette dangling from her fingers. "Come here," she said.

We walked across the street and began to stammer out an explanation. "Well, see, here's the thing. We're spies. We have notebooks! We're writing down what we see, so we're really just protecting the neighborhood!"

Unexpectedly, she said, "Oh my gosh. That's fabulous. Tell me all about it. My name is Natalie." And that's how we met our new best friend.

Every couple of days, maybe two or three times a week, we would climb the rock wall, scoot across the street, and knock on Natalie's front door. She'd come out, always very flamboyant and dramatic, saying things like: "Girls, let me tell you a story." We'd sit on her front porch, and she would entertain us.

She would say things like, "You know I was born on leap day. I only have a birthday every four years. I'm only fifteen years old."

One day she said, "Girls, I need you to help me wash my cat. He's a witch's familiar. He got into some trouble last night."

Another day, pulling keys out of her pocket, she said, "Shall we swim in Mr. Hamlen's pool?"

What magic was this? Absolutely we shall!

We changed into our bathing suits and met her at the pool gate. The keys worked! (Apparently they were best friends, and we weren't breaking in. We just didn't know that at the time.)

Natalie sat down on a lounger and said, "Girls, you can't just jump in the pool. You must make an entrance. Jennifer, your last name is Cobb. Stand up straight, like an ear of corn. Show me your ears. You're corn. Suzanne, be a potato. Squat down. Potatoes have eyes. Show me your eyes." Suzanne squatted down to form the shape of a round potato. I stood there, straight as an ear of corn.

Then she said, "Okay, before you jump in, you must say, 'Where's the butter?'" So we stood there–well, Suzanne squatted there–and said with such conviction, "WHERE'S THE BUTTER?!" Then we jumped gleefully into the pool. Natalie laughed, and we laughed, and it felt so good to be a kid and to laugh with your best friend. So it became our new weekly routine. She would take us to the pool. We would scream, "Where's the butter!?" and we would laugh. It was special, and it was just the three of us.

Summer ended. School started. We didn't see Natalie very much after that.

The next summer, we were thirteen. We went to the Yellow Rocket Arcade instead of Natalie's front porch. We went to the Racquet Club pool instead of our neighbor's pool. We were too grown up for that. We drifted apart from Natalie, and eventually Suzanne and I both moved away.

About eight years ago, my mom called and said, "Hey, did you read the paper? Natalie died." I went online to pull up her obituary. There was that smile and that salt and pepper hair and those big earrings, just like I remembered her.

But then I started reading the obituary, and it was not the Natalie that I remembered. She was a widow. She had three kids. They'd had their own children. She was a grandmother with three grandkids. She had been an accomplished artist. She was an airline stewardess.

You know, her grandkids are probably close to my age. I hope they know how fantastic their grandmother was. I hope they believed she was born on leap day. I hope they've heard the story of the two neighborhood girls she took under her wing and the generous gift of that last magical summer when we still believed in witch's familiars, and a simple dip in a pool became a memory that lasted a lifetime.

Listen to Jennifer Tell Her Story Live:

LaTASHA MOORE

"Congratulations!"

Why do people congratulate me for something a dog can do?

"Good job! You laid down, opened your legs, let a man enter you. Repeatedly thrust his pelvis back and forth, while you may have given a moan or two. He busted his nut. You got up. Cleaned yourself off and returned to bed. To find him already asleep, partially snoring. Smiling, with all kinds of nasty thoughts in his head."

Wow! Bravo. That took a lot of effort and thought, right? Wrong! So why are folks so happy and proud of me for something all kinds of humans and animals are doing day and night? Having sex. Something that can lead to developing new life. One that will seem to change mine almost overnight.

But what about my life? I don't want it to change. I was doing just fine. But I guess one could say I only have myself to blame. The fault is mine. And that's true. The decision was mine to have sex with no protection or contraceptive. And even mine to keep the child when I discovered my monthly visitor was past due.

Nonetheless, I think I'd feel this way in any circumstance. Whether I conceived the child my way or what some call the "right" way, I'd still be upset. Because the changes I'm about to undergo don't sound fun for any woman at any age. Whether it's . . .

> The religious woman who saved herself for marriage.
>
> The woman who is only going through this because she's a sex slave.
>
> The girl who is about to birth her sibling, while the mom or step-grandmother acts like she doesn't know.
>
> The woman who has undergone every fertility option, and the last one gave her hope.
>
> The young girl who was at that wild age whose wild ways have finally caught up.
>
> The woman who is carrying her secret lover's seed as a result of the two months she and her husband split up.
>
> The woman who knows her child is her husband's but that won't stop the beatings.
>
> The loose woman who is going to have to put several men through DNA readings.
>
> The older career woman who will boldly raise a donor's seed on her own.
>
> The woman with no major worries because she has a village behind her and is not doing things alone . . .
>
> No matter when or how we get pregnant, the troubles we go through are the same. We hear the word, "congratulations" just to go through physical, emotional, mental, and social pain.
>
> Congratulations! Your clothes no longer fit.
>
> You used to have breasts, but now you've got huge, sagging tits.

Whoo-hoo! Be ready to never sleep the same again.

Now when you need a babysitter, you'll really see who your family and friends are. Congrats! How long is your maternity leave? Hope your current job is convenient for the new fam-i-ly.

Yeah! How about gestational diabetes, swollen feet, varicose veins, and fatigue for your enjoyment?

Enjoy finding out if you can hold the family down when your spouse leaves for deployment. There's no "me" time.

My body is ugly now, and after the baby comes . . . who knows?

Did I already mention this is my third time having to buy larger clothes?

No grocery store or errand run will ever be the same.

Folks will ask, "How's your child?" as though they've forgotten your name.

I don't see what everyone is so happy about. Maybe they're happy it's me who deals with these burdens and not them.

And is it bad that I'm upset about the newfound attention? Before the maternity shoots and pregnancy posts, I never got so many online likes. It's as though my individual accomplishments were irrelevant and out of sight. I've lived abroad, won prestigious awards, spoken in front of hundreds. But when, "whoop!" I let a man plant a seed in me, three hundred to four-hundred-plus people act like I've really done something.

Congratulations!

Congratulations?

Congratulations.

Congratulations for what?

I wrote that poem on April 28th, 2018. Just two months and four days before my son was born. My son.

Khari Marshall Coleman.

My son.

Who has a very large head, big, beautiful smile, and hair that is a challenge to maintain. My son.

Whose head is probably so large because he has such a big brain.

I know everyone says this, but HE'S SO SMART.

Seeing him process and problem-solve brings a smile to my heart.

My son.

Who finally made me see what people were congratulating me for.

Being his mother and guiding him through this life is an honor. Not a chore. Knowing the big responsibility he is makes me step up to the plate.

And I do so ungrudgingly. I don't hesitate.

Now, let's be honest. Some children really are burdens, but, God, thank you that my son is not. And, hey, I'm not in a rush for a second one, but I appreciate you for the one I've got.

Listen to LaTasha Tell Her Story Live:

RICK CHANDLER

Several months ago, I picked up the phone, and I made the call to Fidelity, the mutual fund company and brokerage house. It was a call I've been dreading because it made everything final. I got to a customer service rep and explained that my mother had passed away on Thanksgiving, and I was the beneficiary of one of her accounts.

The customer service rep very politely said, "I'm sorry for your loss."

I wanted to say, "Don't be."

See, my mother had dementia for over ten years. For the last eight or so, she hadn't known my name. When you go through dementia, it's death by a thousand cuts. At every visit, I would see this strong, vibrant woman who as a young girl had left the poverty of Appalachia, gone to Washington, D.C., off to nursing school with nothing but a suitcase. I saw this woman go from something big to just a little bit less each time. It was terrible to watch. By the end, I was just empty.

But I wasn't going to tell that to a customer service rep. She's not my friend. She's not my therapist. So I just said, "Thank you."

The process was very easy. She took down some information. My brother had already given the death certificate over.

Finally, I asked the question that I'm a little embarrassed to say I really wanted to know more than anything else: "Is there any money left in her estate?" And there was. Not a fortune, but enough to buy a nice car or take the family on a great vacation. I couldn't believe that that was the case. My brother had been managing my mom's affairs for a long time, and she'd been in the nursing home for almost eleven years. That's not the story of any money being left. I couldn't imagine how it happened. And then I remembered a Thanksgiving forty years earlier.

On a Wednesday, I was home for the big Thanksgiving holiday. The next day, my mother would be making a turkey with stuffing and all the dressing. Now, for you young people, you may not know that stuffing didn't always come in a box—that you would actually stuff it in a turkey with different herbs and spices, then that would combine with the juices from the turkey and make great stuffing. Just wonderful.

My mother didn't have any bread. So, she was going to send me to the store to get a loaf. She handed me $5 and said, "I want you to go to the thrift store and get the cheapest loaf of bread they have. Don't get me any of that gold bread with 147 grains made with buttermilk. That's crap." My mother didn't dislike the good bread, but in her mind, it was just one of those things that people who had something bought to make people who had nothing feel bad. "Get the cheapest loaf they have. Usually, it's three of those for a dollar, but I only want one loaf. You may have to pay thirty-nine cents. You may even have to pay forty-nine." I thought, *I'm going to drive ten miles to go save a dollar for a loaf of bread?* But you're not going to win that argument with my mother.

I got in the car and went to work at Coleman's market. Now, Coleman's was a small farmer's market I'd worked at through high school and while at community college. It's about seven car lengths wide, two car lengths deep. And when I walked in, I immediately went to work because it was the Wednesday before Thanksgiving, and they were swamped. I swept the floor, manned the cash register, brought produce in from the cooler. And all while I'm catching up with the Colemans, just having a great time.

After forty-five minutes, I say, "Hey, Mr. Coleman, I need to leave. My mom sent me for a loaf of bread to make stuffing, and I need to get back home." Big cigar in his mouth, he said, "Boy, just take a loaf of bread." I hesitated. Mrs. Coleman, who was standing behind me, knew why I hesitated. You see, they were from Appalachia, too, so they understood the value of a dollar. They knew what hard times were like. They knew that those hard times were always around the corner. And while she would never buy that loaf of bread for herself, she was more than happy to sell it to you and make more money.

She just said, "Boy, Rick, take the loaf of bread. You've been working for the last forty-five minutes." As I was walking out the door, Mr. Coleman put me to work for another fifteen minutes so that he could get that even hour out of me.

Then I went home. We had a split-level house. You come into a little vestibule, you go downstairs. That's where my bedroom was, along with the basement and the door to the garage. Or you go upstairs to where the other bedrooms and the kitchen are. So I went upstairs, put the $5 on the table next to the kitchen, and put the loaf of bread down on the counter.

My mother asked, "Where have you been?"

I said, "I stopped by the Coleman's."

And then I heard it. *Thud, thud, thud.* My mother was marching down the stairs, down the hall. I tried to sneak by her and barely made it down the first flight of stairs to that little vestibule when I heard, "Gosh darn it." She didn't say, gosh darn it. "I told you to get the cheapest loaf of bread possible." She came storming out of the kitchen, looking down at me at the bottom of the stairs. "You boys don't understand the value of a dollar. I'm paying for your college, and you're out wasting money on this gold bread." I just looked at her scared, my eyes big as saucers. A twenty-year-old man, still scared of his mother.

And then she did it. She took her hand, took a big chunk of that loaf of bread through the plastic, ripped it out, and threw it at me. Now she's screaming, her face turning red, spit coming out of the side of her mouth. She's throwing chunks of bread at me. I'm down there dodging the bread, actually, more dodging her stares. As the bread goes by the chandelier, I'm looking to see if there's actually gold up in there. Finally, she stops to take a breath.

I said, "Mom, Mom, the Colemans gave me that bread."

"What?"

"Yeah. You know how Mr. Coleman is? He's always going to put me to work. He gave me that loaf of bread."

My mother looked at me and said, "Well, that's different. Isn't it?"

She took stock of the situation. She looked at me. She looked at the bread on the floor. "Where is my money?"

"Mom, the $5 is right there on the table next to the kitchen," I said.

She picked it up. Then she looked at the whole situation, and she said, "Well, we're still going to need a loaf of bread. So I want you to go to the thrift store and get the cheapest loaf possible."

I wanted to tell the customer service rep at Vanguard about that loaf of bread and my mother and the Colemans and the holidays, but I didn't. She's not my friend. She's not my therapist. I wanted to tell her my brother had done a great job managing our mother's affairs. And I wanted to tell her that the money we inherited wouldn't be used to buy a car or go on a vacation, that it would probably be inherited by my children because my mother did teach me the value of a dollar. But I didn't tell her that either.

I just said, "Thank you. You've been very helpful, ma'am."

She said, "You're welcome. Is there anything else, sir?"

I said, "Yes, ma'am. I just want you to know I miss my mother."

Listen to Rick Tell His Story Live:

SARA BROWN

I hate it when people ask me where I'm from. It's not because I don't feel a sense of place in all the cities and states that I've lived—it's because if I were to answer it honestly, I would say I'm from my mother.

My mom made me who I am. She died when I was sixteen. But that fact alone isn't what makes me who I am. It isn't who she is.

She was the oldest of five kids in her family. She graduated high school and moved out into the world. She dated, worked in NYC, and eventually met and fell in love with my dad.

When I was old enough to do the math, I realized that my mom was pregnant with me when she got married. She used to remind me that it was my fault that she didn't fit in her wedding dress—one of many ways I was and would continue to be a "pain in the ass."

Over the years, my parents fell out of love and parted ways. When I was five, they divorced. It was expectedly tumultuous. We lived with my mom full-time and saw my dad on weekends and holidays. But from that moment on, it was me, my sister, and my mom. She and all others around us referred to us as "the girls," with air quotes and all.

Mom went to nursing school full-time with two young kids. When we were sick and stayed home from school, we didn't really stay home. We went to class with her because she couldn't afford to miss it. I had a notebook dedicated to her nursing classes, where I would pretend to be a student and sometimes ask questions. One time, I even got one right.

As independent as she was to raise us on her own, she wanted to be closer to her family—her brothers, sisters, nieces, nephews, and dad. Eventually, she decided to move us back to the same small town in New York she left many years earlier. My sister went to her elementary school, and I went to her middle and high school. I even had the same history teacher in the tenth grade. My mom joked that she was the most qualified because she was so old she'd lived through most of history anyway.

I was your typical teenager, full of angst, rebellious, listening to my music too loud, and slamming my door too hard. But my mom ignored the lesser sides of me and instead tapped into the good.

She wanted us to have the relationship that I think all mothers and daughters want—the Lorelai and Rory on *Gilmore Girls*—where we would talk about everything openly. As I got older, I became less willing to share details of my life, and my mom became more anxious to learn what was going on. As she was trying to pull in closer, I was pushing away. I'd always kick myself for not being more willing to have that relationship, knowing that I wouldn't have it forever.

The first time my mom was not open with me was when she got sick. When she told us she had cancer. She didn't tell us how bad it was even though she knew. In many ways, it was a gift that we moved back to New York. We had family close by and a social network. I would occasionally miss school and drive her to her doctors' appointments when I had to. She tried to find humor in the situation and even got a wig to match my red hair color experiment. I think she rocked it more than I did.

We were at my aunt's house for a few nights during one

of the hospital stints I had come to expect every few months. I knew when my dad walked in that something had changed.

My dad lived in North Carolina with my stepmom and their brand-new baby. We went and saw my mom in the hospital. She loved Hugh Laurie, Dr. House, so I brought her a *Time* magazine that had him on the cover, expecting her to be able to flip the pages as if she were just at home reading on the couch. But she couldn't. The last thing she said to me, as she held my hand, was that she was sorry she disappointed me by not making it to my high school graduation, a goal I'd later learn she had set for herself. We didn't even make it home from visiting her in the hospital by the time we got the phone call.

Life changed pretty quickly, and I have continued to live my life as if she were still here, also acknowledging the fact that she's not. She would've pushed me, the same way I probably push myself. Not out of disappointment but because she knew I was capable of more, just like she knew she was capable of more, rising to the occasion in so many important milestones of her life—when she was a single mom, putting herself through school with young kids, making hard choices to move to give herself and her family a support system.

My mom set this precedent for me to live a life that is both independent and deeply connected to those around me. How could anyone who instilled these values be a disappointment? The thread that runs throughout her story is selflessness. Being a single mom is an act that requires nothing but selflessness, a trait she maintained while also pursuing her own passions. When you don't have a live-in partner, there is no tag-teaming picking up kids from soccer practice or someone staying home so that the other parent can go out. You're all in, all the time. Even though she might've cherished the time to herself when we were with our dad, there were always tears when we left and tears when we came home.

I know my mom dying of breast cancer makes her a statistic. I know that losing my mom in high school makes me a statistic. But I was never very good at statistics. If there's any way I can honor her on Mother's Day, it's to show her strength.

So why do I hate it when people ask me where I'm from?

I hate it because the story isn't something that can fit in a five-minute networking chat. It doesn't fit on a line in a grad-school application. It's hard for me to answer the question without wanting to give the full answer. So, the honest answer, and the answer that I'm most proud of, is that I am me because of her. I am from my mother.

Listen to Sara Tell Her Story Live:

CRYSTAL C. MERCER

This is a truth that I haven't shared with anybody but a few people close to my circle, 'cause it was so deep and intimate and sacred and painful . . . but the beginning started really beautifully.

I was in love with a man for thirteen years. I met him in high school, and we were just good friends. We began dating after graduation. I was eighteen years old, and this person that I essentially spent my twenties with, and right at the top of my thirties, really taught me a lot about being in a monogamous relationship and helped me form what I wanted as a woman. Sometimes that was him, and sometimes it wasn't, but when it was, it was sweet.

Around my mid-twenties, we decided that we wanted to have children. I mean, we were together, we figured that we were going to be together for the rest of our lives, and we didn't need a ceremony, or paperwork, or other people's approval to start the family that we wanted. But it wasn't as easy as we thought it would be.

I had six miscarriages.

The hardest one was an ectopic pregnancy that I experienced while I was teaching school in Baltimore. My guy was a military guy, enlisted in the Air Force. It was a time that I felt very alone because he couldn't get enough leave to come in time. The situation was sensitive and very critical. My brother had started a new job, my father was sick—his cancer came back and my mother had to tend to him—and my friends didn't have enough money to make the emergency trip. So not only did I lose my baby, but I went through that all alone.

What was lovely in our relationship in the beginning started to dissolve, and there was dissension. For me, being in love is like having a piece of sweet candy in my mouth; I'm smiling and happy, and I'm hyper. But between us, that sweetness began to sour. And towards the end of our relationship, there was a lot of infidelity. I thought maybe it was because of my infertility or me putting the pressure on him of wanting too much.

The straw that broke the camel's back was that the person I was in love with for nearly half of my life had gotten another woman pregnant.

I was so angry.

A part of me was angry because he was deceptive. Here we were going back and forth, trying to make the best decisions for our relationship, and he had a whole 'nother relationship, another woman who was carrying his child. There was a part of me that had a slight bit of happiness because I knew that he wanted children, and that hadn't been something that he was able to do with me, and at that point, I was done, to go forth and be free. But there was another part of me that was extremely angry with myself, and I was feeling inadequate. I was angry at him, yes, because of the cheating and the lies, but I was angry at myself because this woman was able to give him something that I couldn't. He wanted a child, but that was something that I couldn't do for him.

I've had this conflict, this turmoil about my womanhood and how I define motherhood because I've had so many miscarriages, feeling like it was my fault because I do have endometriosis, and I do have fibroid tumors, and I have had dysplasia, and I've had half of my cervix removed, and I've had so many surgeries on my womb. It just affected me in a very negative way that I couldn't procreate with someone that I was intending to have children with.

So, my story of motherhood is not breastfeeding on the porch, sipping lemonade, like I imagine, or holding my babies' hands while they're walking across the street, or all of these milestones that even now, at thirty-six, some of my contemporaries are experiencing. My lens of motherhood comes from the desire to have babies, and it hasn't happened for me. So, I birthed this poem:

FERTILITY

My eggs still drop,
But ain't I a woman,
If nothing hatches?
I bat my lashes,
To push back the tears,
They fall anyway,
Recounting every baby,
That passed,
But ain't I a mother,
If I miscarried my children?

It's confusing,
Can't celebrate the woman who made me,
When she rejects me,
Can't celebrate the mother I am,
Because my babies are dead,
But I ain't standing over no graves,
I have to be kinder to my eggs,
One day I looked in the mirror,
And asked,
"Have you told your body today that she will bear a child?"

My answer was no,
But from that day forward,
I tell myself,
"You will give birth,"
"Your babies will be healthy,"
"Your love for them will mend every open wound,"
I say it,
And I mean it,
But if babies never come,
Ain't I still a woman,
If my dreams don't come true?

I'm not in a celebrating mood,
But my eggs still drop,
Every other cycle of the moon,
My hopes still hang in her Fertile Crescent,
My face still reflecting full,
Even in her waxing and waning,
I weep for my babies,
But ain't I a mother, too?

Listen to Crystal Tell Her Story Live:

ROBYN REKTOR

My adoption adventure started with my own implosion, one I never saw coming.

It was Thanksgiving weekend. We ate a lot of turkey and such. We went to a bunch of movies, watched some at home—eight or nine at least. When my family left town Monday morning, as soon as their car pulled out of the driveway, I burst into big, heavy, gulpy sobs. I did not see this sadness coming, and I had no idea why I suddenly couldn't quit crying.

What is wrong with you? I screamed at myself.

I don't know! I answered.

Why are you so upset?

I still don't know! I shouted back.

What do you want?

I threw my hands up in the air.

A family of my own, I answered.

I didn't know where the words came from. But the answer was definite, resolute.

What?

What did I just say?

I was cemented to the couch for the next few hours, mulling over what this could mean. I listed the ways that I could become a mother, both traditional and non. After I thought through all the options, I eventually settled on a plan.

If I was going to become a parent at my age, and solo, there was only one way I would do it.

"I'll adopt from the foster system in my community," I decided out loud.

The next week, I went to an adoption information meeting. The week after that, I started the paperwork.

Once I made the decision to pursue adoption, I had one child in mind. Our coming together wasn't happenstance. It wasn't chance, like the unions of many families who adopt from the foster system, where they answer seventy-five questions about likes and dislikes, and a computer algorithm spits out a match. Not us. Our story started a few years earlier.

For several years, I took my sweet pup to conduct weekly pet therapy at a behavioral hospital for children. There was one little boy out of the many dozens of kids I had met who stuck with me. He had this aura I couldn't forget, sadness layered with sweetness. Maybe it was the way he gently whispered, "I love you" in Daisy's ear as he snuggled into her or the way he hugged her goodbye.

During my existential crisis on the couch, I did what all good Americans do in a moment of crisis. I consulted Google. I typed in, "Kids in Arkansas who most need to be adopted," or some such phrasing. This led me to the Project Zero Heart Gallery that lists the "last chance" kids in Arkansas who are waiting for foster homes or adoption, kids who have either been in the system for a long time or are hard to place for a variety of reasons. There were 144 hopeful faces in the gallery and seventeen groups of siblings on top of that.

And there he was. The boy with the gentle aura who had snuggled hungrily into Daisy's fur. Next to his name was his status: "Available for Adoption." I read every word of his bio as if it held the keys to the universe.

Soon, I started adoptive parent training. After thirty hours of that, I did paperwork. Scores and scores of paperwork. I divulged insane amounts of personal information and shared lots of references. I spent hours gathering all of the required info.

When that was done, I waited.

On April 20, 2017, the email came in with the subject line: "You are approved for adoption." I didn't know whether to cry or celebrate. I did both. The next day, I made an official inquiry on the boy from pet therapy and waited again to see what would happen next. It didn't take long. A few weeks later, I met with his team—a case worker, an attorney ad litem, a CASA advocate, and people who had been involved in his life. They shared the basic facts of his story, the surface details they knew. Their words didn't begin to describe the boy I would later take home.

I left with a mini skyscraper of paperwork, his legal case file, the factual details of his whereabouts, and the recorded narrative of his five years in the foster system. I spent my evenings reading it, dutifully, page after page, line by line. What I saw happen in those black and white lines was startling. His life and his family unraveled over the pages as drugs and bad choices tore the family apart. My heart broke for the little boy who lost his family and for the mother who lost her three young sons.

The next step was to pre-meet him, or in our case meet again. It happened on a day in May at a behavioral institution in southern Arkansas. As I waited for him, heart thumping, knees shaking, he ambled in, and I didn't realize it was him. Gone was the sweet, smiling ten-year-old face. In its place was an almost-teenager, sulking and bulky. I tried to hide my shock.

We spent the next hour in his therapist's office, barely looking at each other, stealing sideways glances, looking away when caught. Our conversation was painfully awkward.

Over the next few months, we spent increasing amounts of time together. An hour at first, then eight. Eventually, he came to my house for an overnight visit, then a weekend. We seemed compatible. And finally, in the beginning of August, on a hot afternoon, I brought home my new bundle of joy. All two-hundred pounds of him.

Like most new parents, I was both exhilarated and terrified. Soon, I was also exhausted. I started falling asleep at 8 p.m., like I had a newborn. Unlike most parents, the child I brought home already knew a few things—how to cuss like a sailor, how to lie his way out of a corner, and how to manipulate his new mom.

My early days of motherhood weren't spent gazing adoringly at my new baby but trying to teach my preteen things I thought he would already know: how to tie his shoes, how to brush his teeth, how to multiply, how to trust, and how to love, or at least try.

We have lots of challenges. He came with many more than his team realized or than had been disclosed or diagnosed. Every day seems to bring a new challenge of one kind or another as we spend our time going to doctors' appointments and all kinds of therapies and trying to get this life together started on the right foot.

We have some great times, too. He has a fabulous sense of humor and makes me laugh a lot. He likes to watch TV, and I'm into some new shows I'd never thought I would enjoy. A big surprise recently was when he wanted to watch *The Count of Monte Cristo* with me. We watched all seven hours of it, in French with subtitles, and he *liked* it! The best part was thirty minutes into it, when he paused the DVD and asked, "Hey, are they speaking another language?" We have lots of moments like that. I'm appreciative of these lighter ones.

Others aren't so easy, and my parenting ideals and goals change by the day, as do my opinions. One day I think, *I can't do this*. The next minute, I think, *I can fight for this kid forever*. Sometimes, I think, *We won't make it*. I would do almost anything to ensure we do. Where we're going next, we don't know. We're doing the best we can.

Maybe the hardest part in all of this is that I'm not the parent I dreamed of being. I'm not patient enough. I get upset too easily. The hopes I've had of being a kind, nurturing mom sometimes get overshadowed by trying to just survive, to stay calm, to not say unkind things when he's being mean. And when he cusses at me like a thirteen-year-old sailor, it's a win if I hold my tongue from retorting in a similar manner.

We don't know where the rest of our story is going, but we are still holding out for a happy ending.

Listen to Robyn Tell Her Story Live:

GUY CHOATE

In 2010, I developed an addiction to ancestry.com. I spent years of my life in front of a computer screen, trying to uncover the mysteries of my historical family narrative.

Things intensified when my father, who was a bit of an enabler in this scenario, gifted me a membership to 23andMe.com. If you're not familiar, that's a DNA analysis company. They mailed me a little vial, and I filled that vial with saliva and mailed it back to them.

They told me roughly three things: First, where I come from and where my ancestral DNA comes from. I'm 96% Northern European—English and Irish. Second, what medical issues I'm likely to have based on my DNA. For example, the average white, American male is expected to have about a 27% chance of experiencing atrial fibrillation, or heart attack. But because of my DNA, I have more like a 38% chance. So I've got that to look forward to. The last thing they tell you is everyone else on the website with whom you share DNA. My Dad sent in his DNA, and we share about 48%. I've got a first cousin once removed who has sent his, and we share about 5.5%. Then, there are literally twelve hundred other people on the website that I share 1% or less with.

After the initial adrenaline rush, my 23andMe account sat dormant for five or six years. Then, in July 2017, I got a Facebook message request from a girl named Kelsey Weber. She said, "Hi Guy, you don't know me, but I'm here with my father who was adopted in 1965, and he's been actively looking for his biological family for the last seventeen years with no luck until just now. We got his 23andMe results back, and he shares DNA with you."

At first, I thought to myself, *This has got to be the most well-targeted and well-executed piece of spam ever*. But then I located my 23andMe profile, and, sure enough, there's Lance Lang, and not only do we share DNA, but we share like 8% of our DNA, more than anyone else on the website except for my father.

So, I send him a message. "Hi Mr. Lang. I'm pretty well-versed in my family history, and I don't know of anyone who has ever spent any time in Indiana. But if you tell me what you know about your biological family, I'll do my best to help you fill in some gaps."

He replies with what the state of Indiana has told him, which is that his parents are both from Arkansas, they were both eighteen years old in 1965, and when his mother got pregnant, she moved to Evansville, Indiana, where there was a home for unwed mothers. She spent her pregnancy there. Once she gave birth, she gave the child up for adoption and then went back to Arkansas, where she worked as a grocery store clerk and attended the Church of Christ. The state told him that his father was eighteen years old and from Arkansas as well. He was one of six children and was raised on a dairy farm.

Well, my grandmother was one of six children and was raised on a dairy farm. I brought up my family tree, which I love so much, on Ancestry.com. I looked at her brothers' birth dates, and I realized that my great-uncle John would have been eighteen years old in 1965.

I email Lance and say, "I think I might know who your dad is, but I don't want to give you any information about him until I have a chance to talk to him." Lance says, "Of course, of course."

Then I call my Uncle Johnny and tell him everything. I say, "Indiana, 1965, eighteen years old, dairy farm, one of six kids." And I say, "Does that sound like anybody that you might know?" And he says, "Well, it sounds like a whole lot of people I know." He names off a bunch of people he knew that grew up on dairy farms.

I was so disappointed because I think very highly of my family and also of my Uncle Johnny, not to mention that I told Lance that this was going to be a non-issue. I figured I was going to tell my Uncle Johnny this had happened, and then he was going to say, "Well dammit, let's get him up here for a fish fry." I wasn't ready for any other reaction.

But Lance was. He said, "You know, it's okay. I anticipated this, and it's all right." And I said, "No, it's not. This isn't the way it was supposed to happen. He's a good man, but this is not the way he would've scripted things. I think I probably just caught him off guard."

It's been fifty-two years that he's been carrying around this secret. He was not expecting, at the age of seventy, for his great-nephew to call him on the phone. We're fairly close, but I've never called him on the phone before. He wasn't expecting me to call and tell him about DNA. So I said to Lance, "Let's give him some time. He'll come around."

In the meantime, Lance and I got to know each other. We sent text messages and emails. We talked on the phone. We watched the solar eclipse together because we weren't far from the path of totality. We became good friends. During that time he said, "You know, Guy, even if I don't end up meeting anyone else in your family, in our family, I'm okay. It feels good to know that I've got you and your wife Liz and your son, Gus. You're the first blood relatives I've ever met, other than my daughters." It was such a powerful thing. He also said, "If John never wants to meet me, that's okay too, but I hope he helps me find my mother because I think she's probably carrying around a lot of guilt for this, over what happened back then."

I said, "Oh yeah, of course. Any time anyone chooses to give up a child, there has to be an element of self-doubt that stays with you."

And he said, "Well, she never decided that. She didn't want that."

The state had told him that the plan was for her to give him up for adoption, but once he was born, she held onto him for dear life for ten days. Only after her parents drove from Arkansas to Indiana and took him from her did she let go.

It was heartbreaking when he told me. It's heartbreaking now.

Long story short, we found Lance's mother. Her name is Caroline, and she lives nearby in Saline County. We found the phone number for her, and he called her. He explained to her his origin story, and she promptly said, "I believe I'm your mother. I can't believe I'm talking to my baby." Of course she wanted to meet him, to see him again. He agreed to come to Little Rock, and he and his wife, Tammy, stayed with my wife and me. He met his mom, and they had a wonderful conversation, and she cried, and he cried. She apologized and said, "I'm so, so sorry," over and over again. "My daddy made me give you up."

Now that I have a seven-month-old, I realize the power of that—I cannot imagine being forced to give him up.

That night, along with a handful of people in my family that I'd told about Lance, we had dinner at our house. My mom, my grandmother, my aunt, and my grandmother's other brother, Gary.

At the dinner, Gary said something profound that I love. He said, "You know, we've been deprived of this relationship for long enough, and, Lance, you've been deprived of this family for long enough. Fifty-two years is too long. If you can stay another day, I'm going to introduce you to your dad tomorrow."

So of course Lance stayed another day, and Gary went and talked to my Uncle Johnny. He said, "John, I had dinner with a man last night that we believe to be your son, and you need to meet him." My Uncle Johnny drove to my grandmother's house where we were all waiting with Lance.

I'm proud to say that he did what I always told Lance he would do. He walked into the house, and he walked across the room, and he hugged his son that he had never met.

Listen to Guy Tell His Story Live:

ANDY VAUGHT

My parents got divorced when I was eight years old. By all accounts, it was a pretty standard divorce. The majority of the screaming happened behind closed doors, and occasionally that screaming would come out in front of me, but only occasionally.

When they told me that it wasn't my fault, I was like, "Oh yeah, cool. It's not my fault." That was helpful.

Splitting up meant that they had to go to different houses, and they moved about five blocks away from each other in the same town of Covington, Louisiana. They got that thing called joint custody. For the majority of the time, I lived with my mother, and then every other weekend and holidays, I spent with my dad.

My dad moved to a townhouse that was in a creepy row of townhouses in the creepy part of town. It had thick shag carpeting and a rickety iron banister that always wobbled when you walked up the stairs. It had a rabid opossum population in the backyard. You'd look out at night, and there'd be these little things crawling up to the window. And he had this strange neighbor named Jeanette who always spoke with an undead nasal drone. Whenever we exited the house, she would also exit the house. And my dad was like, "Oh, well, she goes around to hospitals and pulls the cigarette butts out of ashtrays." I didn't know if that was serious or not. I still don't know if that was serious or not. So, I was pretty freaked out every time I went to my dad's house.

When Thanksgiving rolled around, my mom was like, "You have to go to your dad's house."

And I'm like, "The place is creepy, Jeanette smells, and there are opossums. It's weird." I was also a mama's boy. I'm like, "I don't want to go."

And she's like, "You have to go." So I get in the car with my dad and we drive the five blocks from my mom's house to my dad's house.

I walk in, and my dad has laid out the most beautiful Thanksgiving spread I've ever seen. He had a big turkey. He had little dishes everywhere. He even put autumn leaves around. My dad hates decorating, so it was really sweet of him. But I was miserable. I sat down, had my head down, and was on the verge of tears.

My dad's like, "Are you okay?"

And I just went, "Nnnnnn . . . "

And he's like, "Do you want to go back to your mom's?"

And I said, "Yes."

And he said, "Okay."

And so we got back in his car and drove the five blocks to my mom's house. I go inside with tears in my eyes. My mom says, "What happened?"

I'm like, "I didn't want to be at Dad's house anymore. I wanted to be with you."

I go to hug her, and my mom goes, "Why did you do that?" She goes, "You need to go back to your dad's house."

And I'm like, "I don't . . ."

She's like, "You're going back to your dad's house."

And so we go out, but my dad has since driven away. So we get into my mom's car, and we drive the five blocks to my dad's house, and he's not there.

So my mom's like, "We have to find him."

I'm like, "How are we going to do that?"

We start driving around town. We go to the grocery store. He's not there. We go to the library. He's not there. We go to all the hot spots in Covington, which are none, and he's at none of them. Finally, we wind up on the interstate. Off the interstate, there was a nature trail.

Mom's like, "We're going to try this." So we pull off, and we go to the nature trail, and there's my dad's car, and then there's my dad coming out of the woods. For all intents and purposes, having a really ungrateful son, he looks pretty happy. We go out to him.

My mom says, "I'm sorry."

And I say, "I'm sorry."

And he says, "It's okay." He says, "Why don't we all just go have Thanksgiving together?"

So we all get into my mom's car and drive more than five blocks to my dad's house. We sit down, and we all have Thanksgiving dinner together.

When Christmas comes around, we do it again. The next year, Thanksgiving comes around, and we do it again. So from that moment on the nature trail until today, we've spent every holiday together.

Now my parents are not friends. They don't go to movies together. They don't talk about things. But at least twice a year, they will convene around a dinner table, and we will have dinner together. It's only about two hours. It's never a whole lot of time. And it's wonderful because there's no expectation. There's no more decoration. We don't have to dress up nice. Sometimes we'll go to a movie, but maybe not. Usually, it's just the three of us sitting together and eating.

I didn't realize it then, and I think I only probably realized it last night when another one of the storytellers reflected on my story, but what my parents were doing was taking their own personal baggage and putting it aside for me, which really is one of the greatest gifts somebody can give.

Next week, on Thanksgiving, I'm going to go back to Covington, to my dad's house. I'm going to sit with my parents, and I'm going to thank them for putting away their baggage so we could all spend some time together.

Listen to Andy Tell His Story Live:

RYAN D. DAVIS

I'm from Little Rock, from the South End. I lived on High Street before it was named Dr Martin Luther King, so that's way back when. And so I'll euphemistically say, we were very, very, very *not* rich growing up. And the people around us were very not rich also, so not much to differentiate from.

I was a good student, for the most part, in high school and went to Lake Forest College on a full scholarship. When folks offer you a full scholarship, and you're very not rich, you kind of have to go. And so my parents said, "Well, it looks like you have chosen a college." And I was like, "I didn't, but okay, whatever."

So they sold me on this idea that Lake Forest is in Chicago. And I was like, *Oh man, I get to go to Chicago*, but it's definitely not . . . somebody from Chicago's here because you laughed! It's definitely not in Chicago. It's about thirty miles north of it, in the northern suburbs. It's almost as close to Milwaukee as it is to Chicago, but anyhow. Lake Forest was a very affluent suburb, and I guess the most notable thing, and notable is to be used very lightly here, is that part of *Ferris Bueller's Day Off* was filmed there. Yes, I know, thank you. That's a distinction, dubious even.

And Mr. T bought a house there. He bought the Old Armour house. You know, potted meat, canned hams, the Old Armour house. He completely ruined that house. Just to let you know, we, I wouldn't say *broke in* because the door was open, but we went in uninvited after they were selling the house, and the whole house was an outfitted Mr. T style with either red carpet with white border or white carpet with red border placed over all of the nice, hundred-year-old parquet floors in the house. Mr. T.

Anyhow, being very not rich, I was a bit shocked at the amount of things that people around me had. Lake Forest College was known as a dumping ground for boarding school kids. That is literally part of the profile from *U.S. News and World Report* from some years ago. And I had no context for boarding school. I was like, *Why can't you just stay at your house and go to school like I did?* And so these kids were going on ski trips and all kinds of fancy things that I still can't afford to do.

For holidays, my dad would say, "If you plan early enough, I'll get you a Greyhound ticket." I am disgusted with the Greyhound to this very day for those long and uncomfortable rides. I still have a bit of nostalgia for it but won't ever do it again.

So one year, I was working for a catering company in the northern suburbs of Chicago that paid a very enticing $18 an hour. Then I was told that the Saturday following Thanksgiving, I was going to get paid $35 an hour to work a party that would maybe take three or four hours, but I would get paid for five hours no matter what. It was an offer I could not refuse, being very not rich. I am all of twenty-one years old at this point and just decided on my own that I'm not coming home for Thanksgiving. I'm just going to chill on campus, maybe break into the cafeteria, get some Lucky Charms. If they have bread still out, I'll eat all kinds of toast, and I'll be good. And when I do this catering gig, I'm going to take all kinds of food home. I'll be fine. But I didn't tell anybody. So my dad called late Tuesday night of that Thanksgiving week. He said, "I haven't heard from you. Is this another one of those 'I'm-not-going-to-say-anything-until-the-last-minute things?" And I was like, "What? No, I'm not going to come home. I'm going to stay here and break bread or play dead. You know what I'm saying? I'm going to make some money this weekend." He didn't sound very happy about that. And so he's like, "Well, that's stupid. That's really stupid." He said some other flowery words, and he called me all kinds of names. I love my dad, but he does that.

Anyhow, that Wednesday, the only people on that entire campus were me and my former roommate who was flying to D.C. Thanksgiving morning. He had a Thursday 7 a.m. flight, so that would leave me on campus by myself. I didn't care. I was about to make $35 an hour. So we come upon a bottle of Jack Daniel's, and we commenced drinking and listening to Al Green. Al Green, come on now, Crittenden County Arkansas's finest. So we're listening to Al Green, drinking Jack Daniel's. We kill one bottle, we drink some random beers from the refrigerator, then we stumble out to a nearby liquor store and get another bottle of Jack Daniel's. I know, fancy, fancy.

We may be about two thirds of the way through the second bottle when—now mind you again, the campus is completely dark, completely empty—we hear a knock at the window. I've never sobered up so quickly in my life. Knock on the window, and we are frozen with a, I don't know if it's fear or what. It is a drunken something, and all I hear is, "Boy, pack some clothes and come outside." That's my dad's voice. Yeah, I know. Right.

It's a chemical thing—you can't just get sober from fear. In that brief sobriety, I maybe packed, like, a pair of socks and some sweatpants or something like that, and I put them in a backpack and ran outside. Now mind you, this is me in the middle of drinking and Al Green. I go from that to heading toward my dad's car. I reached for the front door, and my dad said, "No, get in the back. You smell." So I got in the backseat. This is not a story about that ride because I didn't wake up until we got in the city limits of Memphis.

We got into the city limits. I opened my eyes as much as I could with the looming headache, and I saw him looking in the mirror with disgusted disappointment. I mean, for a full, like, twenty seconds, which is a long time. And so I started avoiding eye contact and just closed my eyes back. I wake up again, and we are at the family homestead in Crittendon County, Arkansas, the great metropolis of Earl. I'm sure you've heard of it. Yeah, give it up for Earl. There you go. Denizens of Earl, y'all in the room.

We get there. My family, they're very Baptist. They're some good, just very, very Baptist people, and so they believe in all of the Baptist things, but they also believe in dressing up to go to a living room and dining room for Thanksgiving. I'm talking about, like, dress shoes and slacks and new sweaters and shirts buttoned all the way to the top. I mean, people get really clean for a Thanksgiving meal in the house that usually does not require all of that.

Back in those days, my locks were in kind of a Basquiat-type style. I only had a beard and no mustache. It was, like, a really big beard. And this is before 9/11, so nobody's freaked out about it. I mean, it's just annoying-looking and not too scary. I had jeans that were ripped from about the middle of the thigh to my knee. I don't even remember what kind of shirt I had on, but I remember the looks of disapproval. So in this half of the room, I have cousins and my brothers who are roasting me and having a good time laughing at me. And then in the other half of the room, I have my elders who are looking at me like, "He's going to hell on a scholarship."

There's a den off to the side, so I immediately retreat to the den chair. My Aunt Louis, who is a very sweet lady who cooks very well, knew I liked chitterlings. I call them chitlins. There we go, we got a fan. And so, she knows that I liked chitlins. The smell of chitlins when you are unsober is . . . I just threw up in my mouth right now thinking of it. But she was very sweet, saying, "Do you need some water? You want to go lay down?" And I just kind of didn't really want to be bothered. So it was kind of an odd day. And I was still halfway kind of off at the fact that my dad had denied me this $35 an hour opportunity. But Thanksgiving happens. It's all good. We have a good time. I eventually sober up and start drinking again with my cousins.

So the next day, of course, is Friday, because Thanksgiving is on a Thursday in case you forgot. My dad says, "Look, I'm going to go lay down and go to sleep, and at about noon I'm going to get up, and I'll take you back to Chicago so you can make your money or whatever."

An impetuous youth, I was like, "Dude, whatever. You kind of messed up my whole weekend anyway, but if you're going to do it, do it. Whatever." And I don't think it really occurred to me until a whole lot later in life that as hard a man as my dad was, as free as he was with the profanity, as weird as he was about people hugging him, he was kind of a sweet dude.

We got in the car, and the entire eight and a half hour drive to Chicago, we talked. We talked about some of everything. He didn't have to do it, but he did, and I love him for it.

Listen to Ryan Tell His Story Live:

EMILY WERNSDORFER HOOKER

I have always been a summer camp person. I never understood those kids who got homesick at camp and begged to go home midweek, because to me, camp was the greatest place on Earth. There was nowhere else I'd rather be. From ages eight to sixteen, I spent at least one week of the summer at my Girl Scout camp in South Central Pennsylvania, Camp Echo Trail.

One thing I love about camp is the culture of storytelling. Every camp has legends, tales, origin stories, and songs that are passed on from camper to camper or staff to staff. These stories may be scary, silly, specific to a location, or have regional variants. Camp Echo Trail had its share of legends and myths.

Camp Echo Trail had one story in particular, which I heard for the first time when I was about twelve years old. I was in a small group of girls for the week, and our counselors must have been pretty tired of us, because one night they went to bed and let us preteen campers build a fire by ourselves and hang out for a couple of hours after lights-out.

At the campfire, a girl in my group said, "You guys know that story about Cricket Bones, don't you?"

I did not know this story, and, like most any twelve-year-old who didn't know something someone else knew, said, "Of course I do. But if you want to tell it you can, I guess. Whatever."

And so she began the story of Cricket Bones.

> *Long, long ago, before Camp Echo Trail was a camp, there was a man who lived on the edge of the forest on a farm. He was recently married to a beautiful and mysterious woman who was not from their town. No one knew much about her, but she was beautiful and perfect—a dream wife.*
>
> *She did have one strange habit. Every night after her husband had fallen asleep, she would rise from the bed, whisper to him, "Darling, I need to go outside for some fresh air," turn on some music on the gramophone, go outside, and later return. Now, the man was a hardworking and tired farmer. He was only half-awake when his wife would leave the bed each night, so he did not think too much about her nightly ritual.*
>
> *One day, he casually mentioned to his friends in town that his wife liked to get up and go out for some fresh air in the middle of the night. His friends said, "Buddy, are you kidding me? Fresh air? She has a fella! They are going out dancing and getting into who knows what! She's runnin' around on you!" The man grew suspicious.*
>
> *That night, he only pretended to fall asleep. He lay in bed with his eyes closed. His wife rose from the bed, like always, saying, "Darling, I'm just going out for some fresh air," putting some music on the gramophone, and going outside. The man waited a moment, and then he followed her. But there was no sign of her anywhere. Not on the porch, not in the*

yard, not out in the barn. Then he checked the woodhouse.

He opened the door . . . and screamed, for he thought he saw his wife hanging in the woodhouse. But it was not his wife. It was her skin, peeled off in one grotesque piece as if she had taken it off like a suit and hung it from the rafters.

He shrieked and ran, then turned back to hurl his lantern at the woodhouse, which burst into flames. He grabbed his horse and rode into town as fast as he could. He knocked on the doors of his friends, screaming, "Help me, help me! My wife is a demon!"

The townspeople tried to calm him down and gave him a place to stay for a few days. The man was almost mad with fear and grief. Three days later, against the advice of his friends, he rode back to his farm. He said, "I must find my wife, whomever or whatever she is."

All was still. There was no sign of his wife or her skin. The woodhouse was nothing but a smoldering heap of ash. The man sighed, "I must be crazy. I don't know what I saw, but it couldn't have been what I thought I saw."

He put his horse up. He heard the sound of summer crickets, creaking and squeaking. As he closed the barn door, he suddenly found himself in a tight grip! He struggled, turned, and saw that he was in the embrace of his wife . . . or what would have been his wife, had she been more than bones and ligaments. When she moved, those bones and joints creaked and squeaked like crickets, so he hadn't heard her sneaking up behind him.

She shrieked, "You fool! You have doomed me to this bony form forever!"

His scream was the last sound he ever made. He was never found. But on the old farm, on summer nights like the night he disappeared, you can still hear the sound of crickets.

As a twelve-year-old, I didn't think of all the plot holes or the leaps of logic in this story. I was nothing but terrified by the notion of Cricket Bones, a skeletal, skinless demon wandering in the woods. Thankfully, this scary campfire story didn't hinder my love of camp, and I continued to attend for many consecutive summers, but I never forgot the tale.

One year, I was a counselor in training, or a CIT. CITs spend a couple of weeks at camp learning how to be good counselors. At Camp Echo Trail, being a CIT meant a lot of grunt work and doing the dirty jobs counselors did not want to do themselves. One night, another CIT and I were tasked with setting up and decorating the dining hall for a breakfast event the next morning. We finished about an hour or so after lights-out and started walking back to our cabins through the woods.

We each had a flashlight, but there were no other lights or any buildings near the wooded trail that took us back to the screened-in cabins of our campsite. We were completely alone. My mind wandered, of course, to Cricket Bones, and I heard a stick snap behind us. I whirled around—nothing.

Feigning casualness to cover the feeling of dread rising in my belly, I said to my companion, "Hey, you know that story about Cricket Bones?"

At that precise moment, I heard it clearly: big-band-style jazz music. The kind you would hear on a gramophone. I froze. My friend froze. She said, "Do you hear that music?"

We took off in a dead sprint back to our cabins.

As a twelve-year-old, I was terrified by the story of Cricket Bones. As a sixteen-year-old, I was terrified by the mysterious sound of old-timey music in the middle of the woods, the origin of which I still cannot logically explain. As an adult, I have used my love of camp as a springboard into a career. I now work year-round as a director at Ferncliff—a camp, school, and conference center in Little Rock. I love almost everything about my job, except perhaps one thing . . .

It's those days of summer camp where I'm busy all day long, and I go to my office after the night's campfire has been put out so I can crank out a few hours of uninterrupted work. It's when I emerge from my office hours after the campers have gone to sleep, the whole site is dark, and I have to walk back to my cabin. All I can hear are crickets.

Listen to Emily Tell Her Story Live:

JASON WOODS

In college, after I studied abroad in England, my girlfriend-at-the-time, Melissa, our friend Deboni, and I decided to go to Scotland. We started off in Edinburgh, and it was a really exciting trip for me because I have some ancestors—I've been told—from Scotland. And also, I grew up Presbyterian, both of my parents grew up Presbyterian, their parents grew up Presbyterian. . . and that's where the roots of Presbyterianism come from, Scotland. It was a trip where I could go and explore my roots a little bit, and I was excited about that.

We started in Edinburgh. Every time we would get close to our hostel, we would see these signs advertising ghost tours. I didn't believe in ghosts, so it wasn't scary, but I was kind of curious. There was one ghost tour that really stuck out because people were being knocked unconscious during it. There were newspapers that confirmed this, reputable newspapers like *The Guardian* and *The London Times*, that had quotes from people saying, *Yeah, I got knocked unconscious*.

I didn't believe in ghosts, but I did believe in newspapers, and I didn't really care why people were getting knocked unconscious—I just didn't want to get knocked unconscious myself. So all three of us unilaterally decided we were not going on this ghost tour.

Until . . . the last day we were there. We were all standing by the same advertisement for the ghost tour. I don't know, maybe I was emboldened by the haggis I had tried earlier that day, but we all kind of looked at each other, and I think we all had the same thought: *We're doing this, aren't we?*

We met our guide and the other tourgoers at the appropriate place at the appropriate time, which was about an hour before the sun went down. We started walking around Edinburgh's Old Town. Our guide was a very good storyteller. She told us some pretty gruesome tales. One was from medieval Scotland. Apparently, they felt the need to torture people every now and then in medieval Scotland. One of the ways they would do it was they would put you on a table against your will, and they would put a rat on top of your stomach, then they would put a metal cage on top of the rat. Then they would put a lot of hot coals on top of the cage so that the cage would heat up, and the rat would panic because it needed to get out to survive. And there was only one way the rat could get out, and that was through the soft belly flesh of the person lying on the table. The rat would burrow through.

Another really uplifting story that she told us happened a little more recently. I guess until the 1800s, there wasn't really a sewage system in Edinburgh. People would collect the human refuse in their house, and then they would throw it out the window. But they would give a warning, yelling "gardyloo," which is kind of a bastardization of French, meaning "beware the water." If you heard "gardyloo," you wanted to run out of the way pretty quickly, or your day was about to be ruined.

But while these stories were gruesome and gross, they weren't really scary. We were in the front of the line, and our tour guide would talk to the three of us as we were walking from place to place. When she was speaking to the entire tour group, she had this thick Scottish brogue. But when we were talking to her, just the three of us, it kind of dropped off a little bit. I thought, *You know what, this is kind of cheesy, but I'm into it.* It was fun and a good way to see the city.

We kept walking, and we ended up at Greyfriars Kirkyard, or cemetery. The first thing we saw when we came to Greyfriars Cemetery was a statue of Greyfriars Bobby. Greyfriars Bobby was a dog, a Skye Terrier. The legend is that his owner died when he was a young pup, and after he was buried at Greyfriars Cemetery, Bobby would go to his owner's grave every day for the next fourteen years to take care of him. It's a really sweet story. I don't think it's true. But I appreciated it, as a dog lover.

Then the sun went down, and the whole tenor of the evening kind of changed. Our tour guide said, "Can everybody see those hills over there?" Yes, we could see them. They're pretty tall hills, and they were everywhere in the cemetery. She said, "During the time of the bubonic plague, so many people died so quickly that they didn't have enough room for all of the bodies." So what they would do is they would stack all of the plague corpses on top of each other, put dirt on them, and eventually they would become these mounds that you see. Just mounds of plague corpses.

And she said, "Follow me," and we walked with trepidation over the mounds of plague corpses to the real crown jewel of the evening, the Black Mausoleum. Now, the Black Mausoleum is the final resting place of one Sir George Mackenzie. He was a lawyer. He was Catholic. And his great joy in life was persecuting Presbyterians. My people.

We were still in the front of the line, so we were the first ones to go into the mausoleum. We went into the back, and about thirty people crowded in. Everyone was shoulder-to-shoulder, and it was hot and humid and kind of hard to breathe. So it was nice outside, but it was just disgusting inside. And everybody was shoved in like sardines, except for this space to my left. I'm not sure why no one wanted to stand to my left, but no one did.

Our tour guide started talking about how she was supposed to lock us in the mausoleum. She said, "But I'm not going to do that, because the last time I did that, I was attacked by the poltergeist. The poltergeist strangled me until somebody else got the key from me, unlocked the mausoleum, and got us out. And after we got out, you could see the finger marks around my throat for weeks."

Conveniently, they had just healed. But, you know what, I appreciated the detail of the story. I was into it. And right as she finished her story about her own strangulation, someone in a costume ran out from behind her and yelled. And everybody in the mausoleum screamed and then started laughing. And then the tour guide started laughing. Everyone laughed, had a good time.

And then she said, "But seriously. The difference between a poltergeist and a ghost is that a poltergeist can harm you, and it feeds off of all the nervous energy and fear of all the living people around it. So now that we've stirred up the poltergeist, we're all in danger of being attacked. So here's what you do. If you feel an intense cold emanating from the middle of your body outward, I'm going to need you to take one step to your left or one step to your right because you're about to be knocked unconscious by the poltergeist."

OK. *That is oddly specific*, I thought. But again, I was really into the detail.

She started telling stories about people who were knocked unconscious in the mausoleum, people who had bite marks, who had scratch marks at the end of their evening. She talked about people who were strangled like her. She talked about people who lived on the outskirts of the cemetery who would come home to blood dripping down their walls and to their fine china exploding out of their cupboards in the middle of the night.

I was really engrossed in the stories until something distracted me. It was kind of this breeze, coming in around my shins. And I thought, *That's really weird*. I didn't feel like there was any ventilation in there, and I had been sweating earlier. It was coming from my right, where Melissa was holding my arm. We were so close I think our legs were probably touching. Deboni was holding her arm, and there were thirty people in front of us. And it wasn't a cool breeze—it was a cold breeze. So I looked at Melissa. I looked at Deboni. They weren't bothered by it. Nobody else seemed bothered by it. I thought, *That's really weird.*

And then the breeze circled my shins, moved around the back of my calves, back to the front of my shins again. And I thought, that's not how breezes work. *That's really weird,* I thought, *This doesn't make any sense. I don't know how to explain that.*

And then I thought, *Surely not. Surely not.* But I thought about that warning and about the newspapers, which I did believe in. *Intense cold, OK. Left or right, I mean, OK, I'll give it a shot.* So, I extricated myself from Melissa's grasp, and I took one big step to my left, then one small step to my left, just to make sure. And the breeze went away.

After that, I listened a little more intently to the stories our guide was telling. Nothing else happened to me for the rest of the tour. We left the Black Mausoleum, and our tour guide said she was selling some books. I said, "Yeah, I'm interested in a book. I'll take a book." We talked about the poltergeist for a little bit. Then Melissa, Deboni, and I walked back to our hostel, weaving our way through a whole lot of drunk people having a good time.

I think we started off talking about the poltergeist and the tour and all that, but our conversation probably turned to something else by the end. It was a long walk. We got back to the hostel, and I was going to go back to the boys' room, and they were going to go to the girls' room.

I don't know what possessed me to do this, but I sat down in a chair and I rolled up the legs of my pants. Around both of my shins were bruises. Solid bruises, same spot on both legs that wrapped around my shins, back around my calves, back around to my shins again—exactly where that cold breeze had been.

So I said, "Hey, I have something to share with the group," and told them the story. I concluded by saying, "You know what? Maybe I bruise easily. Maybe I ran into something and don't remember it."

They both looked at me and, at about the same time, they said, "No, you know what happened."

Listen to Jason Tell His Story Live:

RYAN McGEENEY

There was a time when I was young and in love with a woman who just needed some cats in her life. We had married in the summer of 1999 after having met in a singles periodical, corresponded for about two years, and spent fewer than thirty days in each other's presence.

Despite what you may gather from this reckless snapshot of our relationship, I had some real caution about getting cats, for a couple of reasons. One, I am reasonably allergic to dander and didn't really fancy a house full of cat hair. The other thing is, I hadn't really had a pet since I was about eight years old, and that had gone poorly. I don't want to get real lost on this one, but suffice it to say that between an eight-year-old who doesn't know shit about raising dogs and two parents who are real checked out, pretty soon you're just going to have a dog that barks all the time and tries to bite everyone. And that is how, in 1983, you ended up taking a pretty short drive to whatever was the opposite of a no-kill shelter.

But cats are adorable, right? So my wife set to the grindstone of the internet and arrived at a compromise: the hairless cat. As it turns out, there is such a thing I've since come to know as the Sphynx Rescue Society, but typically if you're buying a Sphynx cat, you're buying it from a breeder. You're not getting it out of the back of a pickup truck next to a basket of peaches in Yellville, Arkansas. If you're going to go to a breeder, you might as well go big. So we drove to New Orleans, and we bought two thirteen-week-old sisters from the same litter. We named them Flannery and Sippora, packed them in little carriers, and set out on our way back to our home in Tampa, Florida.

A few hours into the drive, the sedatives wore off. The cats began literally cat-erwauling. Then, we made our first mistake as new parents. We thought, *Let's let them out of their little carriers. That will chill them out.* Immediately, one of them gets on the dashboard, right above the steering wheel, and the other gets under the brake pedal. Neither of these are ideal at seventy miles an hour, but somehow we survived and arrived in Tampa to begin our new life as a happy cat family.

You know how most cats, when they're born, are cute and kitten-ish and curious, then they turn six months old and don't give a shit about anything for the rest of their lives? Sphynx cats are not like that. They are engaging and personable and fun, pretty much their entire lifespan. And these two were delightful.

Our house had a real shotgun quality to it, and they would rumble from one end to the other, like a herd of tiny elephants. They had a lot of Siamese in their lineage, and so they chattered all the time. Like they had their own language. It was worrisome. You begin to become concerned about conspiracy and uprisings.

A few months after we adopted the cats, the terrorist attacks of 9/11 happened. I was in the Marine Corps at the time, so I was real busy for a couple of years. Real gone, real deployed, real out of the country. Just two years after that though, my second enlistment came to an end. My wife was sick of being a military spouse and pretty tired of Florida. I had somehow made it seven years, still had all my parts and most of my marbles, and just decided not to push my luck anymore.

So I cashed in my chips, went to college, finished one degree, then another. We ended up back in Kansas, where we had both grown up. Now, you may remember that once upon a time, you could just get a liberal arts degree in any old thing, and pretty quickly after graduation, anybody would hire you and just train you in what they needed you to do, and, just like that, you're in the middle class. Well, all of that magical bullshit came to an end around 2008, about a year before I finished my degree in journalism. So, I was as pleased as punch to get offered a reporting job in Northwest Arkansas, which was about a three-hour drive from Lawrence, where we were living at the time.

My wife was of two minds about this. One, newspaper jobs have always been mercurial, and there was no sense in her leaving her university job until I really stabilized. On the other hand, this would definitely get me out of her house, which I think she had kind of come to long for since I had left the military.

As it turns out, what was keeping us together that whole time was me just being gone a lot. I should mention here that my own father has been married six times. Six times. And you know how we're all determined not to become our parents? So there was this definite aspect of, "I will make this marriage work."

We also had the kittens to think of. There were kids involved. Nevertheless, we separated and then divorced, but we did it amicably. So amicably, in fact, that we actually negotiated a joint shared custody of the cats. It's written into the divorce decree.

About every three months, I would drive up and pick up the girls. I paid kitty support. I would introduce them to new women I was dating. (Not too soon though, right? You can't go introducing your kids to everybody you meet off Tinder. That's not healthy for anyone involved.)

I will tell you, one thing that's a good test for a relationship is the cat bathing process. With hairless cats, if you don't bathe them every week, pretty soon you just have two brown cats. So it goes something like this: stalk, capture, swaddle, wipe the little face, clip the nails, clean out the ears, then release and defend yourself. Then you got to do it again, 'cause there's another one who's been watching. This is not for the thin-skinned or profuse bleeders, so that weeded out a lot of ladies.

In 2013, I got a call. It was my ex-wife with a dilemma. Flannery had developed bladder stones. Now, a bladder stone is not an emergency, but if a piece of that stone breaks off and becomes lodged in her urethra, then you have a blocked cat, and that is an emergency.

The vet was saying, "You need this surgery or you need euthanasia, because this is not endurable." As someone who didn't grow up with pets, I had once laughed at stories of people who paid real money for surgery for domesticated cats. I mean, this is not a working animal. What kind of investment is that?

But having these cats really changed me. There's something about the repeated process of pouring all your affection into an animal that you're maybe getting 10% return on that really builds that up in you. Pets don't understand what they're doing to your possessions, your house, your bank account, or your time schedule, and cats, especially, do not give a shit. They don't care, but you learn to love them for the love they can give back, whatever the percentage of return is.

So on the call with my ex-wife, I was like, "How much money are we talking about here?" She said, "A thousand dollars." I didn't even blink. I said, "Do it. I'll send you half."

The surgery was successful. They went on to live their little cat lives.

Shortly after that, I moved to Little Rock, following a woman who had become my second wife. She loves it when I introduce her that way. (It's great. Try it sometime.) But the move doubled the drive time to Lawrence, and by then, the cats were like fifteen—and that's not fair, you don't uproot a fifteen-year-old cat every three months.

So that was the last I saw of them for a long time. Then, last October, I got a text that said, "It's just time." The cats were closing in on nineteen years old. Sippora was riddled with tumors. Flannery barely had the energy to glare anymore. When they were at their healthiest, they weighed nine or ten pounds, but then they weighed six pounds, and then five, and then less.

On their last day, Sippora had a bit of chicken. Flannery slept through breakfast. And off they went. Those girls were born to the same litter. They spent their entire lives together, almost twenty years. They were cared for by a very small number of humans, and they went out together.

We should all be that lucky.

Listen to Ryan Tell His Story Live:

LYNNE FAY

I found my dog, Snow, right after I realized I was going to prison for ten years. Not a literal prison, but existential prison was enough. I knew there was no hope for my marriage, but I couldn't leave until my then five-year-old daughter was much older. So I would be living in a lonely house with a silenced soul and a man I could not talk to, in separate bedrooms, for the next ten years. My romantic life was over at the age of thirty-four, and who knew if I would ever find another partner, on the far and unknowable side of this gray and bleak landscape I was about to walk alone?

We lived in New Mexico at the time, where I had relocated with him as he built his career. The day of my marital epiphany was perhaps the worst day of my life. I sat in the driveway and sobbed, clutching the steering wheel after a useless marriage counseling session. We were radically incompatible and had already been married for seven torturous years.

Not long before that epiphany in the driveway and the clanging shut of the prison door in my mind, both my cat and our family dog had passed away. My grief for my cat was so intense that there was no way I could adopt another cat, but I did want another dog, and I knew the dog I wanted. She would be a dark, short-haired dog who looked like a wolf. I liked my dogs like I liked my ideal lover: beautiful, a touch of poetry in the soul, maybe a little melancholy, non-conformist, and utterly faithful.

But unlike my ideal man, I could search for my ideal dog on Craigslist, and there she was! I called the number for this four-year-old dark, short-haired dog offered out of a private home for adoption. Soon, I was there with this high-strung, vibrating owner who was close to tears the entire time.

"Why are you giving Snow away?" I asked.

"We didn't know she would get so big," she said, looking away and shifting in her chair. "We had to keep her in the backyard, and then we adopted this Pomeranian to keep inside, and it made Snow sad."

You don't say, I thought. Is there any worse torture for a pack animal than being kept in the backyard while another dog makes love to your family in your house?

I patted the dog who was delighting in her brief time in the house and rolling on her back to show her vulnerable belly to the world. Her beauty was stunning. Imagine the Egyptian God Anubis with a glistening, dark jackal head, elegant, tall, rounded ears, and a long, wild nose. She had been drawn in Egyptian art thousands of times before she ever took this mortal form—the myth-haunted spirit hound. Her name was Snow, but she was black. Her nervous owner told me that the name was a joke and implored me to keep it if I adopted her. I said I would, and I said I did want to adopt her, which made the owner start weeping in earnest.

"Will you take her now?" she asked.

"I think I should," I replied gently, "but why don't you come over to my house tomorrow night, and you'll see what a lovely home she has and that she has truly hit the dog jackpot. I think you'll feel a lot better." I brought Snow home in my lap, and her thirty-pound body felt just the right size for it. She looked out the window and whined but tucked into the curve of my body and took comfort.

The next evening, as agreed, the owner came over. Snow had been in my house for twenty-four hours, petted and loved. I sat down on the couch in the living room. The owner sat down on the other couch, ten feet away. Snow looked at us for a moment, then she lay down at my feet.

The owner said, "Snow," her eyes wide. Then she said, "I guess we were just holding you till your real owner came along."

From the moment Snow came to live with me, I had to explain her name to everyone she met. A friend suggested that her name should really be Shadow, because she never left my side.

A prosaic male friend of mine whose family owned a chubby and domestic Miniature Schnauzer once looked at her, lying at my feet, her head raised in museum silhouette. Surprised by his own senses, he murmured, "Snow is a beautiful dog." She didn't bark much, and when she did, it was muffled and subtle. Even more curiously, when she got excited by this rolling toy truck, she would make a strange noise that sounded like, "woo, woo, woo, woo, woo."

When I mentioned this noise to the vet on her first visit, he took a long look, taking in her head, her ears, the single wrinkle on her brow. "I think she's a Lab/Basenji mix," he said. Basenji. Suddenly, her Egyptian presence was more than my dreaming. Treasured by pharaohs, Basenjis are one of the world's oldest breeds and closer to wild canids than any other. For this reason, full-blooded Basenjis are specialist dogs: aloof, semi-wild, and hard to train. But I had hit the dog jackpot in Snow because the Lab blood had blended with the Egyptian to make her as black as Anubis and as kind and gentle as Hathor, the goddess of love and motherhood.

For a decade, Snow went with me. The road of my dead marriage was as grueling as I expected despite the joy of raising my daughter. It grew harder when, five years down, I moved to Arkansas, leaving my female friends behind in New Mexico. The isolation was total. Only teaching drama at a local school kept me engaged and alive through my students. But the lonely silence was still there, deep down, waiting for me, and it took me every time I walked back into the house. Still, Snow was there, in the house, walking with me literally every step of the way. At night, in my separate bedroom, she would lie next to the bed. I could never get her to share the bed, but when I hung my arm down over the edge, she was so close I could touch her fur.

In 2017, my daughter and I moved out. In 2018, the divorce was final, and the thousands of steps along that road had finally led to the far side and freedom. By 2019, Snow had a dusting of white around her muzzle and limped painfully, where she had once bounded four feet off the ground through the grass. Her eyes had blued with age. Her hearing had dimmed. I diapered her tenderly for the last six months of her time with me. Her last vet was as taken with her as I was, charmed by her sweetness and depth of spirit.

In the end, I lay on the floor with her in the vet's office, her head pillowed on my arm, and summoned every moment of joy she had ever brought me, so I could send her off to her own freedom with the full and strong heart she deserved. "You're a good dog," I told her again and again, stroking her as her eyes closed for the last time.

She was truly well-named, I realize now. As the fallen snow that gentles the bleakness of winter, she softened the more agonizing edges of my life for ten years. The bitter cold of that journey was blanketed by her presence, as she fell on the empty spaces and filled them with her faithfulness. The craggy, black branches that lined that lonely road were covered by the soft powder of her love for me.

GLENDALIZ TORRES

I am originally from a small little island surrounded by a lot of water called Puerto Rico. So, I am Latina. I was raised in Boston, Massachusetts.

In the 1970s, in South Boston, we had race riots. My brothers were forced to go to other schools and there was forced busing. I remember running home from school because the white kids were chasing me down just because I was different. I remember going with my mom to look for an apartment and her having the door slammed in her face and being told that they didn't rent to spics, nor did they rent to women with no husbands. That kind of left something in me.

What I was absorbing was really difficult because I didn't know who I was. I didn't know, Am I *black?* Am I *Puerto Rican?* The Black people were like, "You're Puerto Rican." The Puerto Ricans were like, "We don't know who you are."

At home, it was a very Hispanic household. I was raised, not with messages about college or all these things that I was going to do, but with messages about what it meant to be a woman in the United States. Do you go to college? No. You have a career. I was raised basically to be a homemaker. That was, like, the best.

The way I processed this was that I had no value. I had no value being Black. I had no value being Puerto Rican. I had no value as a woman. I started developing, in my head, these voices that said, *You have no value. You're not worthy. You're not loved.*

I pushed on, and I developed this attitude of "It's me against the world, because nobody's coming to help us or to help me." I was being told, "You keep your head down. You do what you got to do. Don't bother anybody, and you'll do fine." But those people who were doing that were doing nothing, and I wanted to be Mary Tyler Moore. I wanted to be that girl and throw my hat up in the air. I wanted to live in Manhattan and have that cute apartment. Those were my dreams, but I knew that I couldn't have them because I had no value. There was nothing that I could give. That's what society told me.

I pushed those little voices to the back of my head, but I still carried them with me, and they stayed in my attitude. I did a lot of good things. I did have value, but I still couldn't see the value in me. I have three beautiful children that I made and gave birth to, without an epidural. So I was a badass, but in my head, I was still functioning with that *What can I offer my kids?* mentality.

I moved to California with that baggage. In 1984, I was married, and after about seventeen years of marriage, I decided that the marriage wasn't really good for me. There wasn't any domestic violence. There was just *I'm going this way. You're going that way. We don't get each other.* So we decided, it's best to divorce. That decision was not what I ever thought was going to be for me, but I pushed through. There were nights when I thought that my kids hated me, but I felt that this was going to be good.

Because I'm a baller like that, I had two jobs. I thought I was an awesome mom and a good worker, and I wanted to help people. I wanted to do all these things to make myself matter. Then, my ex-husband moved back to Massachusetts. I was left with my three children, and no sooner did he leave than I lost one of my jobs.

When that happened, I was like, "Okay, I just got to make it work." It didn't work because I kept falling back and falling behind. Then, those voices started to come back up in my head. After my divorce, I lost the house that we lived in, the home that I tried to make for my kids. We were homeless for the first time in my life. In California, being homeless was no big deal. There are lots of parks, a lot of things to do. I just never thought that would be me. So we had to find a place to live. I did have a car, but it was a real struggle because I was that person that kept it together and suddenly it wasn't together anymore. So, I push forward. That's what we do, we push forward.

They have homeless assistance where they pay for a hotel that you can stay in for the amount of time they allot that you can be homeless, which is about two and a half or three weeks. The only places that we could live for three weeks were on The Strip. If you've ever seen a strip, you know its rent-by-the-hour motels and women working the streets at night mean it's not a good place to lay your head or to have your kids. I had never been away from my kids, but I spent a couple of nights there and then I said, "You know what? I'm going to ask family to take my kids."

It's family, but you don't want family to see you like that. They couldn't take all four of us. So I asked, "Can you guys take my kids in?" It's a lot to ask. Some of my family members live on Section 8, so they could get evicted if I'm there. You don't want to be a burden, so you just have to carry it on your own.

DHS workers told me that they would also help me with my first month rent and my deposit. Again, there was a catch. They would only allow me $600 rent, and they'd pay a $600 deposit. Now, I don't know if you've ever been in California, but $600 rent is going to get you a little hovel in the hood, which is what I had spent all of my life *not* doing. I didn't want my children to live there. So again, I felt like a failure. I failed my kids, again. I wasn't worried about how other people saw me. I was worried about how my kids saw me. I was worried about how I was going to damage them for the rest of their lives.

I eventually started to get it together, and I found a place. A really nice landlord said, "It's $650, but I'll lie for you and say it's $600, and then you just give me the other $50 every month." So he did that, and my kids seemed to like the neighborhood we lived in because they could pretty much hang out all day, but I was still struggling. I could feel myself going into a depression. I could feel those voices, at times, taking over my every thought, *You're a failure. Your kids hate you.* I was really doing my best, but my best, it wasn't good enough.

In the process of being homeless, I lost my other job, but on good terms. They said, "Once you get back on your feet, if we start hiring again, you can come back." I said, "Okay. I needed to focus on getting my kids to school and making sure that they're okay." Working almost sixteen hours a day, I couldn't do that.

So, I got everything together. We were living there for a couple of months, and I went back to work. My healthcare package allowed me to go see a therapist. In my family, we were raised not to tell people what was going on in our house. "You're seeing a therapist? Talk to your mom." Like my mom has it together enough to tell me what I should be doing. In some instances, that support might come from your community, your family. That's that village, but sometimes that village is really fucked up. In my head, I was thinking, *I'm in deep trouble here*. Emotionally, I was a wreck. Mentally, I was a wreck.

I decided, *I'm not going to be that person that's going to say no to help because I have two daughters that are looking at me every day to see my next move, and I'm hoping that they will live their lives with me being their example*. So, I went to a therapist, and she's awesome.

I really didn't want to open up, but the minute I sat down on her couch, I told her my life story in about thirty minutes. I was crying, and she just kept giving me tissues. I think we went through two boxes. Then, after an hour, she said, "I think I need to see you twice a week." To me, that was a life raft, because I thought, *I get to come to this couch and just spill everything and then SHE gets to rearrange it for me and tell me what to do*. I thought that's what was going to happen.

The second time I saw her, I knew what to expect. I think I had cried a lot of stuff out. (Actually no, because I'm standing up here crying now.) I was prepared to be honest with her and just tell her everything, but what happened was that every time I would tell her something, it came out like, "This is what they're doing to me. This is what the world is doing to me." I didn't know that those thoughts that I had in my head, those voices, had been taking, had been taking away my power, from the time that I saw my mom get disrespected, from the time that I saw my brothers running home, from the time that I was running home, from the times that I was told that I couldn't get a job because they do not hire niggers at Woolworth. (They're out of business now, thank God.) All these things form armor. We need it to protect ourselves, but nobody ever teaches us how to take the armor off. I wanted to take it off.

It took me being homeless, me hitting that rock bottom, for me to be able to look up. Before that, I wasn't looking up because I was seeing the world as my enemy.

The therapist taught me how to ask myself the right questions. Every time that I told her about something that happened to me, she would say, "Well, why are you letting this happen to you?" I'd say, "What do you mean why am I letting this happen to me? I have no control over this." She'd say, "Really, is that true?" She got paid a lot of money, and all she really said was, "Really, is that true? Is that true for you? Is that really what you believe?" So basically she had to teach me how to get rid of that belief system that was created a long time ago. She was giving me the ability to take back my power. She was giving me the ability to say, "I am somebody, and I have a lot to give, and I have value."

My daughters got to grow up knowing that they're valuable because I found my value. I found it, and it didn't matter if I was homeless. It didn't matter if I was divorced. It didn't matter how many children I had. It didn't matter whose daughter I was.

What matters is that I am here, and I am valuable. I have the ability to change my life. Every single thing that I thought would make me happy, or make a difference, or bring me joy—every little thing was inside of me the day I was born. I just had to find it.

Listen to Glendaliz Tell Her Story Live:

BAILEY GAMBILL

Note: Names have been changed

I was sixteen when I was raped.

It was December, and my boyfriend and I had just broken up. I still wanted to go to the high school winter formal. Some girls and I decided that we were going to go together.

Brock and James came up to us as the dance was ending, and they said, "Hey, do you want to go hang out?" We were like, "Sure." So we went, changed clothes really quickly, and jumped in Brock's vehicle.

As we were driving, one of the girls got a phone call from her mother, who said, "Hey, something's up. I need you to come home." We teased her, "Ha, ha, ha. It's very funny. You have to go home." We dropped her off. As we were on our way back, the other girl got a phone call. Her mother said, "You need to come home." The girl said, "Ugh, but why?" And her mother said, "It doesn't matter. You need to come home. Something is off." So then it was Brock, James, and myself. Brock said, "Hey, I need to go get gas." So we drove to the gas station.

As we pulled in, he parked at the very back—the darkest part of the parking lot, far away from the door and the gas pumps. He put the car in park, turned around, looked at me, and said, "You have two options. You can have sex with me, or you can walk home."

I nervously laughed and said, "What is going on?"

He said it again, but more sternly this time: "You have two options. You can have sex with me, or you can walk home."

I looked behind me, and I saw the overpass that we just drove over. I realized, *It's eleven o'clock at night, and it is dark. And it is a long walk home.* I hoped that whatever was about to happen was just more to make a fool of me than what's true.

As I turned back around, Brock had gotten out of the car, opened my door, grabbed my arm, and started pulling me out of the vehicle. He repeated, "You have two options. You can have sex with me or you can walk home."

I turned back around to look James in the face. I've never seen a face of such terror in my life. He was opening his wallet and handing me cash. He said, "Go in, and buy whatever you need."

I don't remember picking up my purse, taking the money, and walking inside, but there I was, standing in front of a section in the gas station I had never stood in before or since. I pulled my phone out of my purse. I called everyone I could think of, except my parents, because who wants to call your parents and say, "There's a teenage boy, asking me to do one of two things"?

I grabbed a box of condoms and walked to the cashier. I hoped, once again, that I was going to walk out there and they were going to make a fool of me, because being made a fool of was going to be so much better and have so much less consequence than whatever could happen after. I started walking toward the car in the dark. I didn't even make it all the way to the car before the back door flew open, and I was thrown in the back seat. The door slammed shut, and I heard the locks click.

I look in the front seat and realize that James is now driving and Brock is in the backseat. Brock has positioned himself next to the door that I had just been thrown in. I am already on the other side of the vehicle. I'm still holding my purse, and I'm holding this box, and I don't know what I'm doing. The next thing I know, he yanks the box out of my hand. He throws me on my back. He looks at James and says, "Turn the music up as loud as you can stand it, and drive around until I tell you."

The music goes up, the car pulls out, and now we're on that overpass that I, moments before, had looked over and thought, "I could walk." He pulls my pants down. The more I yell and the more I scream and the more I say, "Please just take me home," the worse it gets, the more aggravated and forceful he becomes.

Finally, he gets so aggravated that he stops. He rolls the window down and throws the condom out. He looks in the front seat, taps James on the shoulder. The music goes down, and he says, "F it. Just take her home."

I am bawling in the backseat. James drops me off at the stop sign at the end of my street. I walk home.

So I had both.

It would be years before I heard the words, "It's not your fault." It would be years until someone said, "What happened to you was rape. This was not your choice."

I vividly remember watching the news and seeing those girls in college that had reported their rapes, their sexual assaults. They were not victims. They were villains, because they took athletes away from their sports. They took people away from their scholarships.

Why wasn't anyone saying that their lives had been taken from them?

I kept thinking, *Both of these boys come from very wealthy families. One of these boys, his family owns a lot of businesses in my hometown. I come from a very poor family. If I told anyone, I would not be a victim. I would be a villain. These boys would lose their basketball scholarships in college, their baseball scholarships. They would lose their spots on the football team. I would be the one who would have been made a fool of.*

It took years. Years for me to say, "What happened to me was not my choice. What happened to me was not my fault."

When I look at those girls now, and when I see what's happening every day on the news and every day around me, I realize it's not their fault. It has nothing to do with what they wore. It has nothing to do with what they said or how they acted. We continue to villainize victims, but it's not their fault.

For everyone who spoke before me and everyone who will speak after me: it is not our fault.

Listen to Bailey Tell Her Story Live:

PATRICIA ASHANTI

Fifteen years ago, I experienced something very, very strange.

I was at home, upstairs in my bedroom, sitting on the side of my bed. It was in the middle of the day, and my children and husband were in the house doing their own thing. I was completely awake, but I had this vision.

I saw myself in this dark place, like a cave. I wasn't alone. My children were there and others. As I started to move, I found my way out. After I got out, I went back. I got my children out, then went back and got other people out.

It is fitting that this experience happened in Helena, Arkansas, because that is where I was born and raised. My mother had eleven children, and I am number nine. My mother was a beautiful woman and had a head for numbers. She didn't have much money, but she always had something when others were in need.

When I left my mother's house, I moved to Pine Bluff to go to school at University of Arkansas at Pine Bluff. I received an accounting degree at UAPB, but more importantly, Pine Bluff is where I received Jesus Christ as my personal Lord and Savior. While there, I developed a very special belief system about marriage and family. I believe that the husband, or the man, is the head of the family in a marriage.

It is with this belief system in mind that fifteen years ago I sat on the side of my bed. I envisioned myself in a cave, finding my way out, leading my children out, and leading others in my community out . . . and I was perplexed. It was very disturbing to me, because at the time I was happily married. I thought, *This cannot be right. If we were to be led out of a dark place, we would be led by my husband. He is the head. He is the leader, not me!*

As a matter of fact, I felt guilty and embarrassed for even thinking that I could be the leader.

What I did not know at the time was that five years later, I would be the head of my family as a single mother of four children. And I *would* lead my children to a healthier environment.

Three years after that, I would become the founder and CEO of Delta Circles, a nonprofit organization that supports families to get out of poverty by examining a poverty mindset and its impact on individuals and the community.

Five years after that, I would lead a group of women from the Arkansas Delta to formulate a Women's Savings Group called WIN (Women Increasing Net Worth). With it, they would move from a place of struggling from year to year to setting saving goals and achieving them for three consecutive years.

Three years after that, I would lead the formation of a young men's investment group . . . the children of WIN. I would help move them from a future of living paycheck to paycheck to being men in their families that understand how to manage money, how to save money, and how to invest in stocks.

And all these years later, I realize that I *am* a leader! I am not just trying to make a difference. I am not hoping to someday make a difference. I AM making a difference! My desire and challenge now are to make a greater impact.

When I think about my challenges with income, I realize that all of them have not always been due to external factors, such as where I have worked or the amount of money that I have made.

My real challenge was not fully embracing my gifts, talents, and abilities . . . Other people recognized them in me, but I did not fully own and walk in them.

So, when I think back to fifteen years ago, as I sat on the side of my bed, I remember the vision ending with me feeling a tremendous sense of growth and expansion. It was like sitting in a bubble or a balloon and someone pumping air into it. It just grew and grew and grew.

And I realize that my story is not over. As a matter of fact, I am in the middle of it.

I know that everything that I desire as a woman—my physical, mental, and financial health—are all attainable in that place of growth and expansion.

As I *choose* to walk in my gifts and talents as a leader. As I *refuse* to wait for someone else to tell my story. As I *choose* to become an advocate for myself. As I *refuse* to wait for permission to lead.

It's all attainable!

When I reflect on that very, very strange thing that I experienced fifteen years ago, it reminds me that I am, and always have been, a leader.

So today, I introduce to you, Patricia Ashanti, LEADER, and Founder and CEO of Delta Circles!

Listen to Patricia Tell Her Story Live:

CHAUNCEY HOLLOMAN PETTIS

I grew up in a family with fifty-six women and four men. Essentially, we had a whole lot of moms and not a lot of dads.

The women in my family really wanted to be present and a part of their children's lives, but also needed to have full-time employment because the world agrees you need light, water, and gas. So, my family became this ongoing group of women-owned business owners. I grew up in daycare centers and family-member-owned restaurants, hair salons, you name it. My mom was an independent grant writer. I'm a fourth-generation, woman entrepreneur. So, thank you.

My first personal experience with my good friend entrepreneurship was when I was about twelve years old. So, I'm in middle school, and I try out for the dance team. I make the dance team and am super excited about it.

I go back to my mom and say, "Mom, I made it. I got selected."

She's like, "Great. Congratulations. I'm so proud of you."

I say, "Thanks. So the dues are due in about three months, and drill team costs $600."

She says, "Okay, no problem. You're responsible for raising half of that."

I say, "What do you mean? I'm twelve. That's a lot of money. How am I supposed to do that?"

She says, "Figure it out."

So, I try a couple of things, and nothing's really working. Saving chip money doesn't really help. I go back and say, "I can't do this. How am I supposed to do this?"

She says, "Let me tell you something: If there's something you want in this world, you're responsible for making it happen. I'm responsible for helping you and supporting you, not doing it for you."

After I try a couple of other things, I decide on candy. I'm twelve. My world revolves around candy. I'm going to sell candy. I go to Sam's, buy a ton of candy, and then decide I'm going to go door to door in my neighborhood and resell it. I come up with two big problems there. First, walking takes a long time, and it's not fun. And second, this is taking too much time to raise $300. So I think, "Where is there a group of people at one time that I can sell candy to?" School.

I pack up my operations and start selling candy at school. My classmates and teachers are my customers. I remember very vividly being late for school one day. The bell had rung. I'm super late, and I'm trying to run, and the security guard catches me in the hallway.

He says, "Hey, you. Where are you supposed to be?"

I say, "I'm supposed to be in Ms. Wilson's class. I'm on my way."

He says, "Okay, you need to hurry up. Get where you need to be." So I turn around. Then he says, "Hey, you."

I say, "Yes, we already did this."

He says, "Give me, I'll take two Snickers. Give me a Snicker."

I do this for about a month. It's going really, really well. One day, my mom gets called, and I have to go to the principal's office.

I go into the office, and they say, "Listen, we're really excited about the initiative that she's taking, but it's starting to get distracting, and we really think it's unsafe that a twelve-year-old is carrying this much cash. We're going to have to shut her down."

So, I closed the doors on Sweets, Inc. and had to stop selling my candy. (Sidebar, I find it super ironic that two months later, the school opens a snack shop. They got rid of the competition. But that's fine.)

My second experience with entrepreneurship is when I'm fifteen. I have a best friend, and she's having a birthday, and it's time for her to have birthday cards. Because she's important to me, I want the perfect greeting card for her sixteenth birthday. I'm faced with three problems. Very few of the cards look like my skin tone. Even fewer of those cards are for our age group. And none of those cards sound like me.

I go back to my mom and say, "Hey Mom, I got this great idea. I want to start a line of greeting cards for Black teenage girls."

My mom says, "All right, okay. Why do you think you should do this?"

I was like, "Well, I write poetry already. It's basically a poem."

She says, "All right, I need a business plan."

I say, "What the heck is that?"

She says, "Figure it out."

I go straight to Ask Jeeves. I look up examples for a business plan and create a seven-page thing.

I take it to her and say, "Listen, here's my business plan. But I have a question. Why would you make me write a business plan? Everything I looked up said this is for banks and investors."

She says, "I am the bank." And she says again, "If there's something you want to do in this world, it's your job to figure out how to do it. It's my job to help you, not to do it for you."

She read my business plan. It was terrible, but she funded Harlem Lyrics, and a month later we had our very first eight cards. We got into Kroger's pretty much immediately. We got to know Walgreens pretty quickly after that.

Two years later, we start other stationary and school supplies. If Black teenage girls didn't see themselves in greeting cards, they definitely didn't see themselves in school supplies.

Harlem Lyrics is doing great and picking up some buzz. We were in *Black Enterprise* magazine and *CosmoGirl* magazine a couple of times.

About five years in, we get a call. Someone says, "Let me just tell you how much I appreciate your cards. I'm a mother of two teenage girls, and them seeing themselves in these greeting cards means so much to me."

I say, "Oh my God, thank you so much. Thank you for calling."

She says, "I'm sorry. I buried the lede. I'm actually a buyer for Macy's Department Stores. We wanted to invite you to come out and pitch your products to possibly have them in Macy's."

Now, it's really exciting. We fly out a couple of weeks later, and we pitch to Macy's. The pitch is only ten minutes, but we do the whole song and dance. We have like $3,000 worth of set-up. We're pretty proud of how it went, and she says, "We really liked it. We'll be in touch in a week."

The longest week of my life. Finally, we get the call. I pick up the phone, and she's like, "Hi, Chauncey. Listen, you had a phenomenal pitch. You couldn't have done anything different. I wouldn't suggest that you change anything. We loved it. But I'm sorry, we're not going to be able to sell your products in our stores."

I say, "If we did everything right, what happened?"

She says, "Well, Jim is the buyer for the stationary department in Macy's, and he just didn't understand the product. I'm sorry I asked you to come out here. Thank you for your time. There's nothing else I can do."

We got off the phone. I cried profusely, as one would. Then, at some point, I say to my mom, "How do we save this? "

I call the buyer back and say, "Quick question. You said you were a buyer for Macy's, right? What do you buy?"

She says, "Junior girls apparel."

I say, "How about this? Give me one month to come and pitch a line of t-shirts based off the Harlem Lyrics characters. Just give me one more shot. If it doesn't work, no harm, no fail."

She says, "Done."

So we design a line of t-shirts based on those same characters they loved so much and go back to pitch again. When I'm done, she says, "Sold." For about three years, my products were in thirty-three Macy's stores in New Jersey, Chicago, and all five New York boroughs.

What I realized is a thing I've called from that day forward "the Jim effect." She said, "I realized I had two problems when I pitched to Macy's—*Jim* and *He*."

Since then, I've helped women start their own small businesses. Entrepreneurship made me who I am. It taught me nothing is insurmountable. Nothing is unlearnable. Nothing is unteachable. And there is absolutely a way to make a way out of no way. I've helped women find their own voices through entrepreneurship. Women who are single moms that just need a way to make ends meet? I've helped them find financial independence. Women who are doing fine financially, but they've been moms or wives their whole lives, and now they just don't know who they are? I've helped them find individuality and social independence.

These women find their empowerment and their individuality through entrepreneurship, just like I did as a kid that needed to sell candy. Just like my mom and the women in my family helped me, I'm so proud to help them make a way out of no way.

Listen to Chauncey Tell Her Story Live:

story-
teller

MACKENZI DAVIS

In the summer of 2000, my mom remarried, and I was uprooted from Crossett, Arkansas, and planted in Eudora, Arkansas. If you don't know the difference between the two, Crossett is very diverse. Eudora is an all-Black town and it was such a culture shock for me because . . . Well, first of all, I'm Black. You can't miss that. But I had never in my life been around so many Black people.

I didn't fit in. I grew up listening to Britney Spears, Jessica Simpson, and Christina Aguilera. NSYNC was my jam. When I moved at the age of thirteen to a small town where everybody grew up together from preschool, or they were family members, I didn't know what my place was. I didn't know where I belonged. I didn't know how to fit in because the reality of it is that there was a part of me that felt like I was not Black enough.

One thing my mom always taught me was, she was like, "You know, baby, don't worry about it. When you get to college, you're going to meet your lifelong friends."

When I graduated high school, I went to Philander Smith College, and I did. I met the foundation of my tribe. The community that Philander gave me was so powerful because I had teachers that looked like me and were invested in me, and I had friends that accepted me for who I was.

When I graduated from Philander, I went to work for an agency. That's when I met Margie and Brenda. They were so pivotal in who I am today because they saw something in me that I did not see in myself because one, I didn't think I was worthy, and two, I had very low self-esteem.

I remember them saying, "Mackenzi, your calling is to be a

social worker." I knew my calling was to be a therapist. I knew that there was so much power in me being for little boys and girls what I didn't see when I was growing up. But I was like, *Mm-mm. No. I'm good.* I became complacent in my role at the agency. I didn't want to further my education, and I was okay with doing that job for the foreseeable future. They kept bugging me, like hardcore bugging me. I had no intentions of getting into grad school. I just wanted them to stop bugging me about it. Despite my negative self-talk and complacency, I finally just took the MAT. Then I applied for grad school, just so they would leave me alone. But fortunately, I got in, and that changed everything.

In 2014, I graduated with my master's in social work and throughout that time, Margie was such a powerful force for me. In 2018, she was murdered, and that was traumatic enough to drive me into therapy. Margie died on Monday, March 26th. I had my first therapy appointment on March 30th, and we buried her on March 31st.

When I first walked into my therapy appointment, that was so hard because I knew, in that moment, that my therapist was going to see me as a broken person. I knew that, in order to give what I needed, I had to be vulnerable. For me, being vulnerable meant weakness, and I had no space to be weak because I carried the weight of everybody that I worked with. Not to mention that I was also fighting my inner self, because I was a fairly passive person who felt like I didn't have a voice. In the moments in which I felt like I could speak up and speak out, my worst fears of not having a voice or just being an angry Black woman were spoken to be true because there were a lot of times when I was the only Black person in spaces that I worked in. In the moments I felt strong enough to advocate for my clients, I was labeled as the angry Black woman, and so I stopped.

The moment that I realized I couldn't advocate for my boys or advocate for the people that I'm here to serve, I knew that something had to change. In 2018, my partner and I started working on a training. It's called "Treating African American Women When the Cape Gets in the Way." It changed my life because I am that African American woman, and I had that cape, but I didn't realize it yet.

In spring 2019, we went to Florida and spoke at the *National Association for Social Workers.* But the pivotal moment of that training was when they invited us to speak at Yale. Y'all, they let two Black women come speak about Black women at Yale! They didn't know what was coming for them because they got all that information.

Imagine spending a year, talking about Mammy, Sapphire, and Jezebel and how we carry that, and how we can remove it and just be who we are and take care of ourselves. It was beautiful. And it was during that time that I realized that my calling was to use my voice, that my calling was to create spaces in which there were not spaces for Black people to use their voices.

Another partner and I held a panel with three Black, male therapists. They were able to have the platform to speak about what it was like for them being therapists, seeing images of themselves being killed in the media and how they were coping with that. It was so powerful to give them a platform to share that.

Following that, by some miracle, I had fifteen Black therapists that were willing to go on this journey with me in which fifteen white therapists allowed them to use the white therapists' Facebook accounts, their platforms, to amplify the Black therapists' voices. And that's a vulnerable space to be in for anybody.

I realized that not only am I here to use my voice, to create spaces that are not seen, I'm also here to create other platforms for other Black people to use their voices. Because at the end of the day, I am a Black woman, and y'all going to hear my voice.

Listen to Mackenzi Tell Her Story Live:

RAH HOWARD

"We'll Get It Right"

My son say he got called a nigger the other day, put me in a bad position, forcing me to contemplate. Explaining racism to a child that's only eight, trying to explain why some people's hearts are just so full of hate. Just goes to show racism rears its ugly head today, saddens me that it's a monster we're unable to escape within our lifetime. That's why I get so frustrated, wondering if years spent marching for freedom was just years wasted.

Because my people still get oppressed on a daily basis. We get murdered, end up on the losing ends of court cases. What up, Trayvon, Mike, Eric, and Emmett? Got me feeling my existence could be ended at any minute by any cop that wrongfully labels me as a menace, decides my skin color makes me worthy of a death sentence. And it's crazy because for a minute, man, I'm ashamed to admit it, that my clean-cut appearance can save me from being afflicted, from racial discrimination to the dagger, called a nigger. Until I got harassed by cops, and saw the world a little clearer. Now I know that my appearance don't make a damn difference whether I'm clean cut, thugged out, light or dark skinned. As long as my skin's pigmented, I'm going to be labeled. God bless the fools who are ignorant enough to say different. They like the lives we're living. Is our imaginations figments? How dare you say the lives we live ain't real because you don't get it? Because your folks wasn't stole from their home, sold in captivity, made personal slaves until they were given their liberty, forced into the ghettos to lead lives in poverty. Go from being kings and queens to the Western world's mockery. I hate when people say, "Don't let the past bother you," when my people presently treated improperly. Got me so full of rage, it's taken every piece of me. To pray for the foolish, conduct myself peacefully. Lord, help me. Let me get up out my feelings, even though it's hard to do when I think of all these killings and all the sad deaths of all these innocent children, forcing me into prayer.

I hope the good Lord sees me kneeling. Yeah. I hope the Lord sees me praying. I hope he hears just what I'm saying. I hope the Lord takes my sisters and my brothers of all different colors, makes us love one another. Pray it takes out the dark, brings us to the light. I pray that in time, man, he makes us right.

I was motivated to write that piece to deal with the anger, rage, and frustration that I felt a few years ago when my son told me that he had been exposed to the word nigger at school. Also compounded by the anger and just frustration I felt from all of the murders of innocent Black men and women at the hands of police in our country. Since writing that piece, over the years, I've continued to write more art, create artwork and films, and make things that are motivated by that. But I got to admit that while I actually like creating that content, there's always been a piece of me that felt like I didn't have the right to speak on these things, trying to figure out if it's even my role to do this, and what *is* my role in the bigger scheme of things?

I don't claim to be an authority in the matter. I'm not any type of activist or political leader. I'm none of that. I'm just a Black dude that grew up in Little Rock that tries to talk about my personal experience. So what I want to briefly talk about is trying to figure out what my role is in all of this, and accepting that, and finding my voice, to actually feeling like I have the right to speak on this stuff.

I have been on this journey for a long time, but I feel like the light bulb just finally went off above my head earlier this year because I got the opportunity to work on a really cool film project that was motivated by trying to teach people about why we're protesting right now—discussing what we want our goals to be out of protest, and what we hope to accomplish. And more importantly, how do people actually find their role in trying to contribute to the fight for equal treatment? I got the opportunity while I was working on this film project to educate people, to talk to a lot of activists and community leaders from around the city.

Amongst them, I got the opportunity to talk to this one brother, Ryan Davis. There was a story that he told me that I thought was so cool. He talked about how, during the Civil Rights Movement, there was a lady who would make bologna sandwiches for protestors while they were protesting. You may hear this and you say, "Bologna sandwich? That's not a big deal. She just made bologna sandwiches." But when you break it down and you think about it, those protestors are out there fighting. They probably get tired and hungry, and when you're out protesting, you can't just leave if you've got something going on. Being able to go over there, get a sandwich, and go back, that's a big deal. So what I was able to take from that story is that this lady, man, that was her part. And the thing is, everybody plays a part or has a role in this movement. There're bigger parts, people that are organizing things and speaking, and a lot of times, that's what we focus on. And we don't pay attention to the small things like the bologna sandwiches that go on. There're big parts and small parts, but there's no such thing as an unimportant part. Everybody has something that they can do. They have gifts, or they have a thing that they can do that can impact the people and the world around them.

I had to take all this information and think about that, do some self-evaluation, and ask myself, *What is it that I can do? What are my gifts?* After doing that, I feel like my thing is creating. That is my gift. That is my God-given ability, to be able to create.

So, how can I use that to help things out? When you think about art, you may say, "Oh, that's not a big deal." I had to get out my head about that, because it *is* a big deal.

With art, especially the role of an artist, a lot of people don't think about that. When artists create art, regardless of whether we're aware of it or not, our artwork is influenced by the world around us. So we're almost like historians in a way, documenting the world. But the thing I think that really makes being an artist important, and makes us important in this whole movement, is a lot of times artists have the ability to touch people's hearts and souls through artwork. That creates a really unique opportunity to convey a message over to somebody and make them receptive to listening to a message or a perspective that they otherwise wouldn't have been receptive to listening to at all. So, it's really important.

I've taken that and come to a conclusion that I'm going to continue to create. And if you're a writer, you should continue to write about and document the world around you. You should talk about your personal perspectives like James Baldwin did. If you're a singer, you should continue to sing and perform and do things that influence the people around you like Marvin Gaye did. The list goes on and on, with the Tupacs and Kendrick Lamars, and other artists that use their medium. I may not have influence like Kendrick Lamar or Tupac, but it's my responsibility to continue to create art with the intention of trying to make a difference or influence with the people who are in my reach.

So, this is my journey to discovering my road as an artist. Going forward, I continue to accept my right to speak on these things and accept my role in this because I'm not just creating art. My intention is to try to create change through my art.

Listen to Rah Tell His Story Live:

JUSTIN BOOTH

My daddy used to tell me he had to pay the other kids to be good, but I was always good for nothing.

By the time I went to prison the first time, I'd already done sets of thirty, sixty, and ninety days at a time in county jail. A couple of times, I'd done full calendar years flat. Most of the crimes that I was guilty of at that time were not having insurance or tags on my car or a driver's license. In this country, it costs extra to be poor. Of course, my addictions didn't help any. I might have had the money otherwise. I can't put it all on the State.

I learned the life hacks of prison in jail. I knew the culture and the lore long before I ever got there. I watched and listened to the older guys telling stories about the penitentiary. I romanticized those guys. I thought they were tragically flawed anti-heroes like characters in books I had read or songs by Johnny Cash.

I retold those stories as if they were my own. I talked about people getting stabbed to death like I had seen it, how the assassin would step over the body without even looking back because he was so cool. I know now they were just as scared as I was the first time, that they couldn't even have a bowel movement for the first day or two because they were that scared. *Now* I know that, right? But at the time, I admired them, and I thought going to prison was inevitable. I considered it a rite of passage.

I knew lots of tricks. I knew how to get two guys to lift a guy up to the outlet behind the television, way up on the wall. I knew how to stick pencil lead into each side of the plug-in and jump electricity across so that we could light a cigarette. I knew how to fasten a can of soda to the air conditioning vent in a wet sock and make it cold after the water evaporated. I knew how to make a spread out of ramen noodles, chips, a meat and cheese stick, maybe a hot pickle from the commissary. I still eat them.

I kept going long enough until I knew that the young men in jail often didn't know their fathers at all. They probably never had anyone tell them what they were capable of, or praise them after a chore was completed. I took on that role. I used it to my advantage. I'd be surrounded by the young guys. It is more important to be able to tell a funny story than it is to be able to fight well. If you are charismatic, you will have the work-out kings all around you. They don't want you to get hurt. They depend on you for confidence and comic relief. It's a boring place and frightening. There is a pecking order, and an educated guess about what will happen next is like currency.

In Craighead County Jail, the misdemeanor side was kind of separated into three sections by where you were charged and your work classification. At a glance, a jailer would know both by the color of our clothes. Inmates wear a sort of rough version of scrubs like healthcare people wear. In the first barracks, the uniform was dark blue. They were city inmates. They would work on the garbage trucks or in the city parks. The next barracks, in yellow uniforms, were county inmates. They probably would work in the jail's kitchen, or they'd clean the courthouse or go to smaller towns out in the county to clean streets or mow. The last guys were dressed in red, and they could not leave the facility. They were the medical profile kids on prescriptions or physically unable to work as a trusty. Some were the knuckleheads and the troublemakers—the people like me who might stick a blanket down the toilet and keep flushing, flooding all of the cells just to piss off the guards who gave them a hard time.

Early on, I had heard that it was better to be a convict than an inmate. It means it's better to be a lion than a lamb. Every time I was ever locked up, I did a sort of Cool Hand Luke impression. I'd say, "Yes, boss. No, boss" to the police, and the uninitiated would think I was some sort of old school criminal that knew everything, and they gathered around. I doled out wisdom and comfort. Doing time is tough, but doing it with no job or purpose is the toughest. Slows everything down and anxieties are magnified.

One time, I heard a rumor that they were going to take the guys in red, the no-goes, and the knuckleheads, and let us go out into the world to work for a couple of days. I asked an officer, but I still couldn't believe it even when he verified what I'd heard. They did take us to town, to the community center. In the colder months, they'd put this sort of a canvas roof over the community center pool. They heated the pool and kept the tent-like roof blown up with positive air force. A big fan and rubber seals around the revolving door kept it blown up like a balloon. Think Jiffy Pop popcorn, right? But it was super heavy and had this hook and toggle system marrying the different sections together. It was intensive labor, hard work. Our hands would cramp, our necks and shoulders ached. For the first couple of hours, I was outstanding. I wanted to get the attention of the civilian supervisor, and it worked. When everybody else went up to the truck to get their little johnny sacks of green bologna sandwiches, a box of apple juice like in elementary school, I just kept working. And that boss man, he came over to talk to me about how hard the job was going to be. I could tell he was out of his depth. I told him I was kind of a shot caller and I could get the others to do anything he wanted if the price was right.

He looked at me with a cocked eyebrow and his face went white. He was scared because he had never been around anybody like me before, anyone who had ever been to jail. He didn't know if I was asking for naked pictures of his wife or his car keys. He didn't know what I was talking about.

I said, "If you throw these guys a pizza party, they'll get after it." And he was amiable to that. I said he could probably get it donated, and sure enough, he did. We worked like towheads. We finally got it all married up, and then we had to drag this canvas tent-like top over huge concrete walls that were around the pool. It was super heavy. And we tried two or three different ways of doing it. Finally, I said, "I'll tell you what, boss man, I'm going to stand up on top of the wall and I'm going to divide our guys into two teams, half inside and the others out. I'm going to give these guys some 2x4s. Outside, they're going to stab up at that canvas and lift it a little bit. And as soon as they do, the inside guys will tug it over and take that slack. We're going to work as a team and get this done."

I said heave, and they'd push up. I said ho, the others pulled. "Heave, ho, heave, ho," walking up and down like something out of an old chain gang movie. They did it. It took a couple of days, but we did it. Then we had that pizza. The boss man walked over to me and asked, "What can I do for you? Something extra because you've earned it." I said, "I sure could go for a Coca-Cola." He said, "Meet me up top." There was a spot above us on the main building where we had looked down at the job two or three different times for a better perspective while trying to decide how we were going to go about things. He had never done this before. I hadn't either, but at least I had some construction experience. I think he was a swim coach or something.

We met up there, and he brought me two Mexican Cokes. I drank them both fast. We looked down at all the young guys who had never done anything right in their lives. They were enjoying the pizza and joking with each other. Clearly, they were happy about completing that job as a team. Maybe they had, for the first time in their lives, done something right. It was one day while I was locked up that I felt like a human being, and the others did too. It was both simple and magical, like a sunset.

Listen to Justin Tell His Story Live:

ELIZA BORNÉ

Sometime during the past year, I tried to remember why my husband, John, became a lawyer. Why does anyone become a lawyer? To make a good living. To have steady, practical work. Maybe to advance the cause of justice.

John and I were married in 2013, a year after he graduated law school. Two years later, he started working on death penalty cases.

Had I known on our wedding day that the contours of our days and weeks would come to be filled in with existential questions of righteousness and mortality? I had not. I had predicted sickness and health, and I was wise enough to expect death and occasional tragedy.

I had not known to steel myself for back-to-back executions, for the media circus that came with them, for the helplessness, the anger, and the grief.

On February 24th, 2017, Leslie Rutledge, the Attorney General of Arkansas, sent a letter to Governor Asa Hutchinson asking him to set execution dates for eight men on death row. Three days later, the governor obliged.

It was a Monday afternoon when John called me at work to report this news. The governor's chief counsel had delivered the death warrants to the Office of the Federal Public Defender, where John works. He had been the one to discover the formal proclamations in the interoffice mailbox.

John and his colleagues got to work drafting a letter to the governor explaining that the execution protocol was deeply flawed, citing botched executions in other states. *If the executions are to proceed,* they wrote, *not only would our clients suffer, but so would our state's image and moral standing in the eyes of the country and the world.*

John emailed me the letter so I could proofread it. Then he sent me a list of dates:

April 17: Bruce Ward and Don Davis

April 20: Stacey Johnson and Ledell Lee

April 24:, Jack Jones and Marcel Williams

April 27: Kenneth Williams and Jason McGehee

I read the letter a couple of times, then I opened my calendar so I could input all the dates. "Did you realize that the first execution is set for the day after Easter Sunday?" I replied to John.

"They don't care," he replied within a minute. "Kill."

The governor did not heed their letter.

One of the many problems with the rushed execution schedule was the burden it put on the lawyers. The appeals process leading up to an execution is so byzantine. There are hearings to prepare for, petitions to write daily, briefs zinging back and forth, and clients who have to be updated every step of the way. It is nearly impossible to provide adequate representation on such a compressed timeline. John told me to expect hell. He'd work around the clock, doing everything he could to advocate for his clients, all of whom had a history of ineffective counsel from their previous lawyers. All of whom had lived in solitary confinement for years, sometimes decades. All of whom were usually reduced to grotesque stereotypes in the media, defined only by their crimes.

Here's what we did know: If the state got its way, at the end of April, eight men would be guided to a death chamber where they would be forced to lie on a gurney and connected to lethal drugs through a vein in the arm or the leg or maybe the neck if the vein was tricky. They would die after a process that was designed to appear clinical and humane, as if a scheduled execution conducted in front of a gallery of spectators could be anything but savage.

As March and April pressed on, John came home only to sleep. I thought of it not like hell but like trauma surgery. An endless triage.

The first week in April, Judge Kristine Baker set a federal court hearing on the execution protocol. John and his colleagues argued that one of the drugs did not properly work as a sedative. Thus, the execution would be a cruel and unusual punishment. Lawyers from the state argued that the executions should move forward. The night before the first day of the hearing, I delivered a lasagna to John at the office. We ate in the law library and talked a bit about what we thought might happen that week in court. We both knew that this would be the last good chance to get a stay of execution. I encouraged John to come home and get a good night's rest. He was starting to get sick from too little sleep, too much stress. Instead, he worked until 2 a.m., came home, and slept for a few hours. Then got up, downed a glass of Emergen-C, put on a suit, and went to court.

The hearing lasted twelve hours a day for four full days. It turned out to be a very revealing week. Among other things, we learned that one of the drugs had been anonymously donated to the Department of Correction, evoking images of a shady parking lot handoff. We also learned that Wendy Kelley, the head of the Department of Corrections, did not seem to have a clear understanding of how these drugs actually worked, a shocking admission for someone with her authority. The hearing ended late on Thursday night. On Friday, Damien Echols, one of the West Memphis Three, was joined by his friend Johnny Depp for a rally at the Arkansas State Capitol. By then, Arkansas's so-called "rush-to-kill" story had become international news, and reporters crowded the famous speakers, trying to get a good shot.

I took an inventory of the signs. One of them said, CAPITAL PUNISHMENT KILLED JESUS. It was Good Friday.

On Saturday morning before dawn, Judge Baker ruled in favor of the prisoners. The executions were called off. We didn't have time to celebrate. John and his colleagues were back at the office all day Saturday and into the night and all through Easter Sunday, arguing that the ruling should be upheld. Lawyers from the State argued that the ruling should be overturned.

The 8th Circuit Court of Appeals eventually overturned the ruling.

The U.S. Supreme Court refused to stop the executions in a five-four split. The deciding vote was cast by Neil Gorsuch. It was his first vote as a U.S. Supreme Court Justice.

Four men were executed at Varner Unit, three received stays of execution, and one, Jason McGehee, was granted clemency. Ledell Lee was executed on April 20th, four minutes before his death warrant expired. It was the first execution in Arkansas since 2005. Ledell maintained his innocence from the day that he was arrested until the night of his execution, more than twenty-four years later. His last meal was Holy Communion.

Jack Jones was executed on April 24th. After he was administered the sedative, he continued to move his mouth and gasped for air for more than twenty seconds, showing signs of consciousness. That night, the governor released a statement that the execution had been "flawless."

Marcel Williams was also executed on April 24th. This one was especially hard because the funny and kindhearted Marcel was one of John's favorite clients. A week after he died, John and I went to his funeral to celebrate his life and mourn his pointless death.

Kenneth Williams was executed on April 27th. After he died, a media witness who has observed numerous executions reported a disturbing scene: he said that Kenneth had lurched and moved his body on the gurney. One of Kenneth's victim's family members had unsuccessfully petitioned the governor to spare Kenneth's life. That night, the governor said, "The long path of justice ended tonight." Justice for whom, I'm still not sure.

To represent death row inmates is to become intimate with brokenness. Lawyers who work on capital cases return often to this concept.

David Dow, a lawyer in Texas who has represented death row inmates since the late 1980s, puts it this way in his book, *The Autobiography of an Execution*: "Understanding a broken human being in a visceral way means that you are broken, too, at least for a while."

Last year, after our tax dollars paid for the death of four of our fellow citizens, authorized by people elected by voters, I came to understand the sentiment, and I believed it. The system was broken, and we were all implicated. We were all broken too.

Listen to Eliza Tell Her Story Live:

DENISE DONNELL

I got the job because I'm Black. Yep. That was the only criterion.

Some male who was white and able-bodied and heterosexual, some Jesus-following genius, had been spending his time studying the residential trends in our area. He knew that before long, the church in that neighborhood would be filled with folks who are Black. It would follow then, that sooner or later, there would be a whole bunch of Black folks attending the church. Well, at least they would visit. Now whether or not the Black people stayed at the church would be a totally different question. And that's the question we were there to answer. What are we going to do with all these Black people? No one in that room could answer that question, but they believed they knew someone who could—another Black person. So, I was hired, and thus my tenure began.

It didn't take long for all the white folks to realize that no one knew what to do with these Black folks, including me. But these weren't just Black people. These were Black people who were poor. Now, I've been Black since the day I was born, but I ain't been poor a day in my life. I didn't know what to do either.

So, I did the only thing an academician knows how to do. I read a book and took a quiz. I still remember three of the questions:

1) Can you move in one day? *Naw, I can't move in no one day. It takes me two days just to think about how many boxes I need to get started.*
2) Where is the nearest Food Pantry? *Can I look it up in the phone book?*
3) What time do you have to leave the homeless shelter every morning? *Wait, you got to leave a homeless shelter? Where they do that at?*

Needless to say, I flunked that quiz. And in the eyes of all those white parishioners, I flunked being Black, too. They could not understand how it was possible that a person could be Black and not know what it means to be poor. They simply could not figure that out. That led to us trying to come up with some response to the Black folks who were in the room who were poor. Nobody in there knew what to do.

As I was living that experience, the one thing I internalized about race and about my life was that I am not *that kind* of Black person. I am not poor. I will never be unemployed, and I refuse to be a victim of the system. In my mind, I didn't have to figure any of this out for my life. So, I didn't.

I can't even begin to imagine how different my life would be now had I taken seriously the plight of those Black folks I called myself "serving," because something happened to me on April the 28th, a Tuesday in the year of our Lord 2020, that changed my life forever. Somebody put an alert on my calendar for a meeting with my boss's boss's boss and HR. In no universe could this possibly be a good thing. It wasn't.

Once I joined the meeting, I learned that as soon as I hung up the phone, my job was going to end, and that at 6 p.m. Eastern Standard Time that same night, I would be locked out of the computer. Not only that, I must be escorted out of the office and out of the building with all of my personal belongings by close of business Friday.

I couldn't talk. I couldn't walk. I couldn't breathe. I couldn't move. I couldn't think. I couldn't do a thing. As it turns out, I was one of twenty-two of the first round of layoffs in response to the novel coronavirus pandemic that some folks are walking around here saying ain't real. Yeah, tell that to my bank account.

I'm trying to figure out: *What do I do now?* When I walked out of that building for the last time, I did not know what to do. I did not know where to look for a job. I did not know what kind of job to look for. I didn't know how to translate my skill set. I didn't know how to articulate my skill set. I didn't know how to respond to the interview questions. Do I tell them the truth, which would probably mean I'm not going to get the job, or should I lie and tell them what I know they want to hear about diversity, equity, and inclusion just to keep a roof over my head? I didn't know who to list as a reference. I did not know *how* to file unemployment. I did not know *that I could* file unemployment. I didn't know how to find the unemployment office. I didn't know anything at all. It finally dawned on me. I could Google and figure out whatever I need. Just ask Google.

I followed the instructions from the website, the GPS directions to the Arkansas Department of Workforce Services. I parked my car. I grabbed a book from the back seat. I took a number, and I walked to the end of the line. I flipped to the page bookmarked in Isabel Wilkerson's *Caste: The Origins of Our Discontent* and picked up where I left off.

"We are responsible for our ignorance, and with time and open-hearted enlightenment, our wisdom." I kept reading that same sentence over and over again until the words started moving. The words changed shapes and sizes and places until there was only one sentence left on that entire white sheet of paper. It was a question. It dawned on me I had been asking myself every time I looked up and saw a different person standing in line in front of me. That question was, "Is that me? Am I *that* Black person?" *Yes, Denise. That is you. You are unemployed. Your mortgage is in jeopardy. Your car note is due. Your dental insurance just got canceled. Your health insurance is about to run out. Yeah, that's you.*

Maybe that's a good thing. I'm not sure. I couldn't figure it out. So, I thought, *Let me just go back and make sure I'm understanding this*. I flipped back a page to the beginning of the chapter in *Caste*. I thought, *Let me just start from the beginning again, so I can try to understand*. Immediately, the words ran off the page and left me with that same question: *Is that me?* Because I study the Bible, I know that whenever Jesus says something twice, it's meant for us to dig deeper. To see this same question again in my mind means that I missed something the first time.

The question is: "Is that me?" *Yes, Denise. That's you.* What do you mean? Who is me? Who are we talking about?

Yeah, let's ask the question.

Is that you who thought you could fight for the lives of poor people without having any idea at all what it means to be poor?

Is that you, Denise, who thought you were gifted and graced and talented enough to change people's lives without even having a meaningful, ongoing, authentic relationship with them?

Denise, is that you who thought it was okay for you to take positions and serve on boards and give testimony and represent a whole group of folks you don't even know on a personal level?

Is that you?

Yes, Denise. That's you. But that's okay. Life has happened. Life is happening. Life will continue to happen. Maybe now, faced with the reality that so many other people are faced with—people that look like you, people who are you—maybe now you'll learn what it really means to be poor and Black in America. If you learn that, maybe, just maybe Denise, you'll be able to stay in the fight and actually be more effective.

Good luck with that.

Listen to Denise Tell Her Story Live:

GLORIA RICHARD-DAVIS

I was the only Black female in my class of 185 in LSU School of Medicine, class of 1982. I trained in the historic Charity Hospital, founded in 1736. The new Charity Hospital was built in the 1940s, and it was this monstrosity of a building, thirteen floors, over 1,600 beds, with two distinct towers actually designed specifically for segregation. One tower had white patients, the other had colored patients, which is what we were called then, and there was an administration in between.

The patients we took care of were poor and about 75% Black. LSU's faculty and student body were over 90% white. And as a Black female, of course I experienced racism. I was called the N word by a classmate. I was used to all sorts of other terms of endearment, sexism, you name it. When you look at being a medical student in that environment, I really felt powerless. There was nothing that I could vocalize or felt like I could vocalize. So instead, what I did was put my head down. I drove on much like my other Black classmates did, and there were few of us. The cuts, the bruises that we endured, we just had to ignore them in order to survive. I chose a theme song that I played in my head, and it was Gloria Gaynor, "I Will Survive." I'd sing it for you, but I really can't carry a tune, not even in a bucket.

When I think about my career as a Black woman, I really come face to face every day with health inequality. It is an inescapable truth of our daily lives. In college, I started researching heart disease and obesity, and I've continued to focus on health disparity throughout my career. Now, I focus more on disparities associated with women of color.

I joined UAMS faculty in January 2013 as a tenured professor of obstetrics and gynecology. Then, in January 2020, I was really excited to start a new position as executive director for the University of Arkansas for Medical Sciences (UAMS) division of diversity, equity, and inclusion. I've focused much of my career on this, and so it's as if the stars were aligning. When I look at our mission, it is to diversify the healthcare workforce and to really seek health equity in that quest. Fast forward to March and enters COVID.

Originating in Wuhan, China, it made its way across the globe and to the United States—first Seattle, then New York. And the mid-U.S. felt pretty safe, but very quickly it was like a tsunami, like a wave that came across the country into every possible remote recess. There were no communities left untouched. We were in a full-blown pandemic. Corona, or Rona as the kids call her, was disproportionately affecting communities of color. Black and brown people were dying two or three times more than whites. Why?

The very diseases that I researched as a college student, heart disease and obesity, which were also rampant in our community, were also the risk factors that increase the risk of dying from COVID. I was nominated to chair of the Arkansas Health Equity Response Team. As a team, we were charged with applying an equity lens to the disparities that we were seeing impacting communities of color, so to write guidelines and recommendations as to how we could potentially address them. It was also very clear that we had economic disparities, and the gaps were widening.

COVID had laid bare some of the health inequities that we knew existed previously, but we had intentionally ignored them. Same is true of economic disparities. And the two compounded were just escalating the disparities that we were seeing in communities of color. We thought it was bad battling those two, and then enter social injustice and unrest. On May 25th, captured on live video by a seventeen-year-old bystander, we witnessed the brutal murder of George Floyd. Three Minneapolis police officers held him down on cement while Derek Chauvin knelt on his neck for eight minutes and forty-six seconds.

During that time, you could hear him repeatedly say, "I can't breathe. I can't breathe." And then he called out for help from his dead mother. As a mother, and I'm sure for other mothers, hearing that ring in my ears broke my heart. Meanwhile, Derek Chauvin knelt full-force on Floyd's body with his hands in his pockets, very nonchalantly looking into the camera as if it was nothing until George Floyd's body went limp. The world erupted into rage at the inhumane treatment that we all witnessed with our very own eyes.

Every Black person that I know was crushed. We felt every emotion from anger, to fear, fright, and fury all rolled up in one. We all knew this could be any of us. It could be my brother, my husband, my child, and to treat anyone like that is unacceptable.

Our UAMS medical students were, of course, enraged, rightfully so. And they wanted to join the protest. As a faculty and a parent, I appealed to them, "We're in the midst of a pandemic. I'm concerned for your safety. Please reconsider." Some of them went. Some of them didn't.

I was dealing with my own internal struggle. And as a Black physician, what could I do? What could we, our UAMS medical community, do to stand against racism?

In a matter of two days, we organized an assembly of White Coats for Black Lives (WCBL). We asked leadership to give brief remarks and sent out mass emails not really knowing who was going to show up. Noontime, lunch hour, on that day to my surprise, over five-hundred UAMS employees and families showed up. It was an amazing scene to see the mass of people out in support of the Black community, and to take a stand against racism. Our remarks focused on acknowledging racism as a public health crisis that is killing Black and brown people en masse.

Police brutality, we know, is a visible sign of racism, but it's just the tip of the iceberg. When we look at the statistics, there are over 83,000 Black and brown lives that are lost needlessly due to health disparities from racism. We honored the names of the men and women that we witnessed dying at the hands of the police.

We knelt silently, somberly on hurting knees for eight minutes and forty-six seconds. The visual and the experience were powerful. While kneeling, it seemed like forever, and it became easier to imagine what that was like for George Floyd. I heard people whispering in the crowd. "Is it time? Is it time to get up?" I looked at the time, and I shook my head. *It's not time.*

But I thought, *Is it time to end racism?* Yes, it is absolutely time.

In 2021, just as in 1984, I will continue to fight against racism, social injustice, and health inequities, in quest of a just culture and society. As I keep singing "I Will Survive," at least to myself, it feels good to remember the day that many white coats came together to kneel in support of social justice.

Listen to Gloria Tell Her Story Live:

ANDREA TOOMER

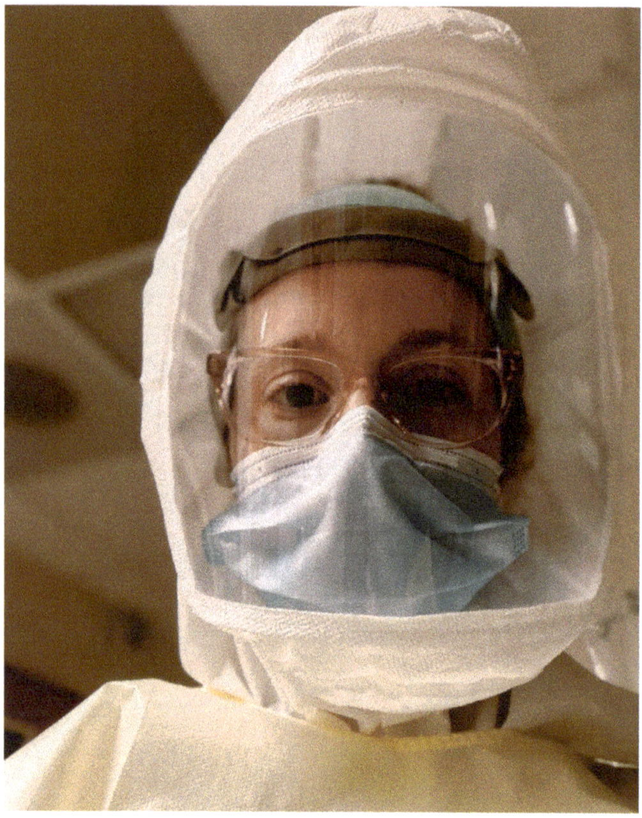

I'm an ICU nurse, which right now means that I'm a COVID ICU nurse.

I became a nurse six years ago for a variety of reasons. When I was a teenager, I volunteered at a local hospital in the ER and neonatal ICU and on a cancer floor. Then my best friend got in a high-speed motor vehicle accident and suffered a traumatic brain injury that kept her in the ICU for months. I spent a lot of time being a friend and supporting her throughout her stay.

Volunteering in the hospital as a ffifteen- to seventeen-year-old, I was probably different from other people my age. I wasn't squeamish or uncomfortable in any of those situations. I just found it really cool to be a part of some of the biggest moments in people's lives and to have the opportunity to help people and make a difference. Maybe that sounds cliché, but it really did give me a lot of joy and satisfaction.

I didn't really know what I wanted to be when I grew up, and I wasn't considering nursing. I was never one of those kids that had it figured out, but I think to everybody else around me, it was probably a lot more obvious that something in healthcare, and probably becoming a nurse, was my calling.

So, I went to nursing school and graduated. I was really excited to play a big role in helping people get better. I went to the ICU to do that, because I found that it would be interesting to really dive deep in, take care of complex patients, and challenge myself. It's something I've really enjoyed doing for the last five and a half years.

Then COVID threw a wrench in my sense of what my job was. Like many other nurses, I went from a regular ICU to a COVID ICU. Back in March, the hospital was empty. We weren't doing elective surgeries. People were scared to go to the hospital. Contrast that with now, when there's not an empty bed in the ICU. We're full. I walk into work and ventilator alarms, monitors, and call lights are going off, and people are rushedly donning and doffing PPE. It's chaos, and everyone looks tired. And you can just, I mean, it's palpable, the exhaustion and despair. You walk into the unit and it's a completely different place than it used to be, and I'm a completely different nurse than I used to be.

In this new role, my ability to connect with patients presents it's own set of challenges. You're wearing a big powered air-purifying respirator hood, or PAPR, and it's blowing air, so that alone makes it hard to hear. A lot of times our COVID patients are intubated on a ventilator, on life support. They have a breathing tube down their airway, and so they can't talk. I'm having to yell for them to even hear me on top of all of the alarms and everything that's creating noise and distraction. Sometimes, they don't understand English, so then you throw an iPad with a translator at it, and a Bluetooth speaker, and you have the volume up all the way. At times, they are able to give you a thumbs up or thumbs down to answer simple questions. They can kind of gesture, but you're not connecting with the same ease that you used to be able to.

One particular example of this new level of difficulty with patient-to-nurse connection comes to mind. I had a Spanish-speaking patient that I was having a really hard time figuring out how to help. A lot of patients try to find ways to pass the time and entertain themselves somewhat. But he wasn't watching TV, wasn't looking out the window, wasn't texting, wasn't FaceTiming, wasn't listening to music. I really felt like, *Hmmm. This isn't right.* Like, *What's going on with him?* He finally was able to write that if he FaceTimed his wife or his kids, he would cry. So that's why he hadn't been on the phone with them . . . He wrote that he really didn't feel like doing anything. That he just felt empty and flat and depressed. Imagine standing there, fully clad in PPE, up to your elbows in life or death situations, reading this.

There are moments when you're the one standing in the room with them, and you're kind of their only support. You are their visitor. You are their family. You are that constant in-and-out person who knows their names and learns things about their personal lives outside of this new COVID ICU world you are both in. It's this role that before COVID, I've never really found myself in—to be people's only connection with the outside. I've seen a lot of patients lose hope with the lack of connection to the outside world, to their old lives, to their families.

We give people clipboards, with pen and paper, and they're able to write basic needs sometimes. As you can imagine, these critically ill patients are so exhausted and suffering so deeply. Some literally write down, "I want to die." Or, "Pull this breathing tube out. I give up." And to be the only one in the room seeing that, reading that, is a moment that I could never have imagined. These are people that shouldn't be in this situation, but they're dying because they have coronavirus.

So you go into work, put on a tough face, try your best to be everyone's cheerleader. But to have to be the strong one, to have to tell these people that they need to keep plugging on . . . it's really hard to do, because I don't know what it feels like to be them in the bed. I just know that a lot of times their fight isn't over yet, and I think it can make all the difference in the world to encourage people, to try and be positive, and to try to give everyone a shot.

But it's hard to be positive, especially in some of these crazy moments that we have been around for. There have been several times that I go into the supply closet to get a body bag after a patient has passed, and we don't have any. We've run out. That's a very strange feeling. I don't even know how to really describe what that feels like, but all of these very emotionally charged things that are happening are just crazy and feel impossible to process.

Before this, I don't think a patient death really ever significantly got to me. I would tear up in the moment, but not drive home from work crying, or cry at work to my friends, or cry myself to sleep. Death was always something manageable, kind of just a fact of my job, and a part of my life, and I didn't really struggle with it. But these COVID deaths are so much harder. They're so much more complex. Really the only people that know what it's like in a COVID ICU—besides nurses, doctors, respiratory therapists, and nurses' aides—are the patients themselves.

Kind of a crazy juxtaposition to all of these things that make it hard to connect, but then we have this connection on the other end that's so intense, and this bond that is so strong from everything that we've been through together in this whole COVID ICU war zone. You've taken care of these patients for weeks, gotten to really know them and formed this bond, and in their final moments you're the only one with them. You're by their side when they're dying. You're holding up an iPad so their family can say, "Goodbye." It's like you're hearing these people's eulogies as they're dying, as their family at home is talking to them, comforting them, sharing memories.

The times that I get upset when patients die now is . . . it's almost every time. It's almost impossible for me not to get upset and not to cry when these people die. The lines have been blurred, and I feel so much more connected to that person than times past.

I've been really grateful for my coworkers, for being able to lean on them. Just like the patients need us, we need each other.

Really, we all need each other more than ever right now. If we can drop the political opinions and personal beliefs regarding this, and just take care of one another, look out for one another, worry about others' safety, things will get so much better.

Listen to Andrea Tell Her Story Live:

NICOLE HELLTHALER

When I was a kid, I was convinced that when you were happy and in love, you or your partner had to die. I specifically remember having to be picked up from a sleepover because all of the girls were watching *A Walk to Remember*, that movie with Mandy Moore where she falls in love with that cool guy from high school, and then she dies. I managed to make it through other Nicholas Sparks stories, like *The Notebook* or *The Last Song*, but not without tear stains on the pages.

I'm tired of this narrative, and I'm tired of the fear that's associated with it. I'm tired of being scared.

Last year, my father died of stage four metastatic prostate cancer. It was a progressive, vicious disease, but it did not define him or defeat him, and it did not define his love story. My dad saw my mom from across the room and said, "I'm going to marry that woman." That part, the movies got right. He swept her off her feet, whisked her away from a man on a motorcycle that didn't treat her right. From then, they were hooked, and they were in it for life.

Growing up, I had the cool parents. My dad could do back flips on the golf course and he taught me back handsprings in the front yard. My mom always made the best food and was, and still is, the kindest person that I know. My friends always wanted to be at our house, if that says anything about the home that my parents created. One of their favorite times, and one of the most embarrassing times for me, was when they danced at weddings together. Now, the times they danced are among my sweetest memories.

When I was a kid, I also remember a time we were sitting around the coffee table, eating takeout. Mom and Dad were arguing. My mom stabbed the fork down on the table really, really hard. It bounced and stabbed my dad in the arm. We were concerned about infection. They went to the hospital and my mom, being a nurse, had to tell her friends that she accidentally stabbed my dad. Like most of their arguments, it ended in laughter and more love.

Once I got to high school, it got a little bit tougher. My dad got really skinny. He started smoking cigarettes a lot. He didn't come home as often. And my parents were always arguing. His siblings even thought he might've been doing drugs, that's how skinny and sad he was. It turns out he was $30,000 in debt. He was gambling, addicted to scratch-offs, trying to fix his problems on his own. He finally told my mom, and it was a really treacherous time, but they made it through. I've never seen my dad cry, maybe once or twice, and one of those times was when he thought he let my mom down, and he wasn't good enough for her. Again, they made it through.

When I was in college, my dad fell thirty-five feet from a roof. He was cleaning gutters, and a swarm of bees came by and knocked him off balance. He shattered his tibia, his fibula, and both of his ankles. This warrior of a man crawled to his car and was able to drive home. He made it to the driveway and passed out in my brother's arms. He hadn't told my mom yet. He didn't want to worry her.

Our house became a makeshift hospital. We had a hospital bed, PIC lines, all the drugs you can imagine. Their love created space for beautiful chaos. My brother and I argued over who got to sit in the wheelchair when we were watching TV.

This was to be my dad's moment. He was healing in more than one way. He told me he thought he fell off the roof for a reason. It was like he needed a reset to be jolted awake. He would grow from this.

Then he got cancer. His disease was treatable, but not curable. His prognosis was about three to five years. We were hopeful at first. It really wasn't so bad that first year. He was able to golf and work, and my parents went out on dates.

It's just that it got worse from there. Cancer fucking sucks. It takes the person that you love and it makes them tired and sad and sleepy and pale. It robs you of family outings and peaceful evenings, because the pain from chemotherapy and radiation is so unbearable. It takes the life that you thought you were going to have, one that includes your dad walking you down the aisle and getting to meet your kids, and crushes it with every lesion that emerges on his brain. It robs your mother of getting to grow old with your father.

Despite this pain, they were never more in love. My mom never missed a chemotherapy treatment or a radiation or doctor's appointment. She was actually a little nervous to go to chemotherapy with him at times, because he made so many people laugh they thought they were going to get kicked out. She was given four months paid leave to take care of my dad. All of her coworkers donated their paid time so that she could have that time to take care of him. They believed in their love. I believed in their love. My mom always made him meals and she fought off insurance companies in order to get his medicine.

It was beautiful to witness. It's just that even love can't save someone's body when it's really, really sick.

When we were hitting the three-year mark, they found lesions on my dad's brain. It was starting to get hard for him to text and to string a sentence together. He was in a lot of pain and was sleeping a lot. Then, one day he was in so much pain that my mom knew she had to bring him to the hospital. He needed the type of medicine that you couldn't administer at home to help ease his pain.

That week is forever seared in my memory. There was laughter. There were tears. My dad altered between sleeping and restlessness, but my mom never left his side. As his death approached, his love was never more bold. He fought so hard against the medicine. Sometimes his will was stronger than the drugs. I was at the hospital all week, but after a while, it just became too painful. I had to go home. My body was breaking down. So I left my parents together. On his last night, they were alone. My father died at 2 a.m. with my mom holding his hand.

I remember when she came home and joined me in bed. I had woken up, knowing something was wrong, the way you can just tell sometimes when big things happen. As she was dozing off, she looked at me and said, "Maybe I'll see Daddy in my dreams."

I don't know why this had to happen in my family. I wish my dad didn't have to die. I wish I could finish this story with a reason why things like this happen at all.

What I do know is that my parents were lucky in love, and I was lucky to witness their love—to be created by it and to embody it. There is a hole in my chest that is never going to be filled. My existence is forever altered. I am different. I will continue to be different. But because of their love, I am brave. I am stronger. I am okay. I'm open to love. I welcome it.

Listen to Nicole Tell Her Story Live:

KAREN HAYES

Karen submitted her piece to The Yarn show two weeks before she died. Mark Hotchkiss, the "library guy," read it in her absence.

My husband was a Little Rock bar musician. His name was Bobby J. Hayes. He had Alzheimer's. He died in 2014. This is not a good way to begin a love story.

Bob and I were married for twenty-nine years. I never planned to marry again. I never planned to DATE again. I'm a poet. I accidentally picked up a beautiful man downtown at 2nd Friday Art Night. I did it with a poem.

The man is my age. An appropriate man. He's a library guy. Maybe he was especially susceptible to poetry. True, I bother strangers with poems all the time, but I certainly didn't intend for this to happen. Admittedly, I did lay the poem directly on him. I set it straight into his lap, looking into his eyes. The poem was light, with some serious bits, and a funny little kick at the end. Everybody likes that poem, including me.

When I was done, he said nothing. He kept looking into my eyes. He took my hand. He took my hand! Nobody except my husband had held my hand in thirty-two years. I mean, really held my hand.

It only got worse. By the end of the evening, I was letting him walk me to my car. As we walked, I steadily explained about being a widow. And not for that long. A year and a half. When we reached my car, he asked for my phone number. Was it too soon? Yes. I handed him my card. Oh good Lord. I was sure he would call before I got on the freeway. I was in no state to talk. Not anymore. I had talked enough.

When I got home, I sat at the kitchen table and poured myself a shot. What if he was married? What if he was batshit crazy? There was at least an even chance he was crazy. He was interested in me. What the hell was wrong with him? He wore glasses. How long had it been since he had his prescription checked? Was his hearing impaired? Could he not see and hear that I was a sixty-two-year-old woman with all the wrinkled and opinionated baggage that entails? And here he was, just lovely. Why wasn't he chatting up forty-five-year-olds?

I called my friend Barbara, who hasn't dated since the George H.W. Bush administration. She was surprisingly helpful. "What do I do when he calls?" I said. "Nothing," she said. "You don't have to talk to him."

He never called. By the next Art Night, I was ready to straighten this joker out. Why didn't he call me? I knew he liked me. Fine. Like me. But quit hanging over me! I stood on the balcony at the Butler Center, a bad-tempered Juliet, waiting for him. Of course he would be here. He worked next door at the library.

When he walked in the door, he didn't look up. I headed for the stairs. I had him in my sights now. He met me at the top of the stairs. We fell into each other's arms.

"I was hoping you'd be here," he said.

I still don't want to get married again, and I still don't want to play the dating game. But love? Oh yeah. Count me in. When this beautiful man and I go to 2nd Friday Art Night in February, it will be our three-year anniversary.

Listen to Mark Tell Karen's Story Live:

CURTAIN CALL

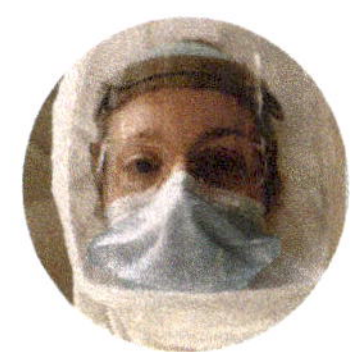

ACKNOWLEDGMENTS

Amplify: We are grateful to those who backed us on Kickstarter. Your generous support has made it possible to publish this book, helping us further amplify our storytellers and their stories. Thank you to Gerard Matthews and 19ninety Films for our incredible Kickstarter video. A special thank you to John Gaudin and Potluck & Poison Ivy for believing in the vision of The Yarn and for serving as our fiscal sponsor and one of our fiercest supporters.

Build: The Yarn could not exist without the brave storytellers who stand on our stages and share their truths. Thank you for sharing your stories to help build the community we all want to live in. We appreciate you and stand with you. The Yarn's dedicated team of volunteers has donated so much of their time and talent over the years. Thank you to Sara Brown, Brad Cameron, Laura Creech, Stacy Cox, Julianne Dunn, David Fischman, Jensyn and Noah Hallett, Melissa Hite, Emily Wernsdorfer Hooker, Amy Hopper, Tiffany Jacob, Omaya D. Jones, Adam Kittrell, Nicholas Manolagas, James Rector, Jessi Rice, Michael Silverman, Ash Steele, Kelsi Stimack, Sara Swisher, Angela Toomer, Ellie Wheeler, Katie Zakrzewski, and Niki Zimmerman.

Create Space: Thank you to Errin Stanger of Arkansas Regional Innovation Hub, Anna Kimmell (formerly of Arkansas Repertory Theatre), the staff of CALS Ron Robinson Theater, Sarah Catherine and Jorge Guitierrez of Club 27, Chris Cranford of Cranford Co., Sally Mengel of Loblolly Creamery, John Hardy and Lee Weber of New Deal Studios & Gallery (who took a chance on our very first solo show), Amy and Matt Bell (formerly of South on Main), Adam and Sarah Farrell of The Joint, and Jason Tedford of Wolfman Studios for welcoming The Yarn into your spaces to build community and amplify these stories and many others. Special thanks to Nathan Vandiver for amplifying The Yarn stories throughout Arkansas on the radio waves of KUAR.

A special thank you to Erin Wood from Et Alia Press who believed in this book from the beginning and has held our hands through every step of the process. She also brought us together with Amy Ashford who has made this book as visually compelling as the stories within it. It has been a truly wonderful experience working with you, and we cannot thank you enough.

OUR PARTNERS

ARKANSAS COALITION AGAINST SEXUAL ASSAULT

*Co-Host of **#MeToo: True Stories of Sexual Assault***

Through collaborative action, ACASA advocates for the rights and needs of persons affected by all forms of sexual violence. We envision a world free of sexual violence in which men and women together assure that all human beings are treated with dignity and respect for their physical, emotional, intellectual, and spiritual integrity.

#MeToo: True Stories of Sexual Assault was produced at the Ron Robinson Theater in Little Rock, Arkansas, on Thursday, April 19, 2018.

arkcasa.org

ARKANSAS REPERTORY THEATRE

*Co-Host of **Neighbors: True Stories of Fences and Friendship** and **The Call: True Stories of Adoption***

The Arkansas Repertory Theatre exists to produce diverse theatrical works of the highest artistic standards. As the state's largest nonprofit resident theatre company, The Rep employs guest artists from across the country and local artists to produce works—created, rehearsed, and built in downtown Little Rock. With a focus on dramatic storytelling that illuminates the human journey, ranging from contemporary comedies and dramas to world premieres to the classics of dramatic literature, their work serves to entertain, engage, and enrich local and regional audiences of all ages and backgrounds.

Neighbors: True Stories of Fences and Friendship (Friday, April 5, 2019) and *The Call: True Stories of Adoption* (Monday, January 22, 2018) were produced at the Arkansas Repertory Theatre's Education Annex in Little Rock, Arkansas.

therep.org

DECARCERATE

*Co-Host of **Barred I** and **Barred II: True Stories of Incarceration***

DecARcerate works to end mass incarceration in Arkansas through community education, smart legislation, advocacy, and by empowering the leadership of individuals personally affected by the criminal punishment system. DecARcerate believes in a state where communities are safe and caring, individuals who cause harm are rehabilitated and reintegrated into supportive communities, all people are respected and treated equitably across institutions, and systems of exploitation and oppression are replaced with ones that are just and create healing.

Barred I: True Stories of Incarceration was produced at the New Deal Studios and Gallery in Little Rock, Arkansas, on Wednesday, January 31, 2018.

Barred II was produced at Cranford Co. Studios in Little Rock, Arkansas, on Thursday, May 16, 2019.

decarceratear.org

HUMAN RIGHTS CAMPAIGN

*Co-Host of **Outloud***

The Human Rights Campaign envisions a world where every member of the LGBTQ+ family has the freedom to live their truth without fear, and with equality under the law. We empower our 3 million members and supporters to mobilize against attacks on the most marginalized people in our community.

Outloud was produced at South on Main on National Coming Out Day in 2016, 2017, 2018, and 2019.

hrc.org

OUR PARTNERS

OUR HOUSE

Co-Host of ***True Stories of Resilience from Our House***

For over three decades, Our House has worked to build a pathway out of homelessness for clients across central Arkansas by providing comprehensive services on a seven-acre campus. Our House aims to be a one-stop shop—providing housing, child care, youth programs, case management, career assistance, mental health services, and more. By working equally with parents, children, families, and individuals, Our House connects clients to the skills, resources, and knowledge they need to avoid or exit homelessness permanently.

True Stories of Resilience was produced at Cranford Co. Studios in Little Rock, Arkansas, on Thursday, March 14, 2019.

ourhouseshelter.org

ROCK CITY RESCUE

Co-Host of ***Stray Love***

Rock City Rescue saves animals from situations that are abusive, endangering, or neglectful and rescue animals in danger of being euthanized at area shelters/pounds. RCR provides necessary veterinary care and treatment to the animals in their care, places homeless and rescued animals into RCR-approved foster homes until permanent homes can be secured, and places rescued animals into permanent adoptive homes. They educate and promote the importance of spaying/neutering and educate the public on how to help prevent animal cruelty and neglect. RCR also engages in other activities related to animal rescue in the community.

Stray Love was produced at South on Main in Little Rock, Arkansas, on Tuesday, February 11, 2020.

rockcityrescue.org

WASHITAW FOOTHILLS YOUTH MEDIA ARTS & LITERACY COLLECTIVE

Co-Host of ***Black Lives Matter***

Washitaw Foothills (WFYMALC) is a multi-media, arts and literacy based collective. We capture oral history and social determinants through interviews, photography, video, and various mediums of art, with a focus on youth development.

Black Lives Matter was produced at Wolfman Studios in Little Rock, Arkansas, on October 23, 2020.

wfymalc.org

WOMEN'S FOUNDATION OF ARKANSAS

Co-Host of ***Striving Forward: True Stories from Arkansas Women***

WFA envisions an Arkansas in which women achieve economic equity and security. Their mission focuses on ensuring economic security for Arkansas women and girls through focused philanthropic investment in education and economic well-being. Through grant making, research, and Girls of Promise and Women Empowered initiatives, the Women's Foundation of Arkansas is investing in real solutions that allow women and girls to move up the economic ladder and reach their fullest potential.

Striving Forward: True Stories from Arkansas Women was produced at Club 27 in Little Rock, Arkansas, on August 28, 2019.

womensfoundationarkansas.org

OUR SPONSORS

HEIFER INTERNATIONAL

*Show Sponsor of **Voices from the Field***

Heifer USA supports small-scale sustainable crop and livestock businesses to build a food system that allows farmers to succeed. Local farms are the future of sustainable and healthy food production, and they can only stay in business if their farms are profitable. Using a community development model, Heifer USA connects farmers to technical experts, suppliers who can deliver a quality service at a reasonable price, and new markets for their goods. The work comes together through a collaboration of three separate entities—Heifer USA, Cypress Valley Meat Company, and Grass Roots Farmers' Cooperative—to meet farmers' needs from farm to table and produce quality products that guarantee a living income. Heifer USA works directly with farmers to improve their processes, offering training both online and at Heifer Ranch—a living classroom where farmers learn regenerative agricultural methods that apply to their farms—and invests in the infrastructure farmers need to support their businesses. Through investment, training, and collaboration, Heifer USA helps farmers deliver healthy, nutritious, humanely-raised food to market.

heifer.org

HOUND'S LOUNGE

*Show Sponsor of **Stray Love***

Hounds Lounge is a locally-owned-and-operated up-scale dog facility where dogs can be dogs and come home really, really tired with the "Hounds Lounge hangover." Staffed around the clock, Hounds Lounge is cage-free, indoor/outdoor, off-leash facility with private, luxury boarding suites.

houndslounge.com

POTLUCK & POISON IVY

Fiscal Sponsor, The Yarn

Potluck & Poison Ivy is a live dinner and storytelling event in Argenta, Arkansas, that invites you to bring your story to the table by sharing a meal and some good ole Southern storytelling. It's a potluck of people, themes, and ways to tell a story, served with a hearty helping of laughter, Southern exaggerations, and even some unexpected poison ivy. Whether it's scripted, unscripted, or an open mic storytelling casserole, this is one picnic you don't want to miss.

potluckandpoisonivy.org

STORYTELLER BIOGRAPHIES

Rhonna-Rose Akama-Makia is a second-generation African immigrant raised in the American South who is passionate about politics and economics. As a trained facilitator, she has facilitated 1,000+ workshops with over 10,000 individuals from various communities, organizations, and companies across the country. She is currently the Director of the Engagement Studio at Think Rubix.

Patricia Ashanti is the founder and CEO of Delta Circles. She is a recent graduate of the Clinton School of Public Service with an Executive Master of Public Service and has a BS in accounting from the University of Arkansas at Pine Bluff. As a proud native of Helena, Arkansas, she has always recognized the need for community service and had a desire to help families thrive. In 2009, she led a community effort which resulted in her becoming the founder and CEO of Delta Circles, a nonprofit organization with the mission of supporting families to end poverty and challenge the way that Black women think about themselves, their finances, and their businesses. In 2014, Patricia received the *Arkansas Times* Visionary Award for exhibiting creative leadership for her work in the Arkansas Delta. In 2017, she formulated WIN, the Women Increasing Net-worth Saving Group, which has empowered women to save collectively and create new financial narratives for their futures. She is an enthusiastic supporter of entrepreneurial leadership and was recognized as a 2019 Community Philanthropy Advancing Equity Award recipient. Patricia serves on several local boards, including the Arkansas Advocates for Children and Families. She works diligently with community leaders to direct the formation of the Eliza Miller Opportunity Hub (EMOH) in Helena-West Helena. She also coordinates the Delta Owned COVID-19 Relief Fund sponsored by the Winthrop Rockefeller Foundation, to provide critical capital needed to maintain and re-imagine small businesses in the Arkansas Delta. Most recently, through Delta Circles, she has established a partnership with the Arkansas Small Business and Technology Development Center, (ASBTDC), to increase small business services and resources to minority and underrepresented communities.

Dr. Marck L. Beggs is a poet, singer-songwriter, professor, and aspiring Buddhist. He is the author of four collections of poetry, including *Blind Verse* and *Libido Café* (Salmon Poetry, Ireland) and a member of the folk-rock bands, Bohemian Sauce and dog gods. Marck and his wife, Carly Cate, both teach English at Henderson State University and live in the People's Republic of Hillcrest in Little Rock. Their household now includes three dogs and three cats. In 2009, Marck was selected as one of the top ten sexiest vegetarians by PETA.

Justin Booth has published seven books of poetry. His latest, *Hookers, Ex-wives, and Other Lovers,* includes beautiful verses that splash down the page like a kicked-over drink. Live, he channels his father's Sunday sermons and sinner's hymns. Not sentimental, this is rather the poetry of flesh-snagging razor wire, Denny's parking lot fistfights at 2 a.m., and passion poems with a heartbeat, more hopeful than ever. Booth is eager to perform with other poets, hear live music, and restore connections. The self-described "outlaw poet" looks forward to the age of sixty and believes then he'll live forever, and he will be able to fly. This strange truth was revealed decades ago by Bernarda Bruja, after he spit in her palm and she mixed in red dirt, laughing nervously. Booth visits her still at a suicidal cliffside cave-dwelling near Huapoca Canyon, Mexico, where he first read to her and they fell in love like only the very young or most foolish do.

Eliza Borné is a writer, reader, editor, and fundraising professional in Little Rock. From 2015–2021, she served as editor of the *Oxford American* magazine. Today, she is the Central Arkansas Library System's Director of Development.

Born in Wisconsin, **Sara Brown** has been working her way back to the Midwest after living in New Jersey, New York, North Carolina, and Arkansas. With an undergraduate degree in sustainable development from Appalachian State, Sara spent her time after college working at an Alternative School in Asheville, North Carolina, and then spending several years at a global nonprofit focused on ending world hunger. A frequent listener of *How I Built This* podcast and supporter of entrepreneurs, Sara was hungry for start-up experience. She got her MBA from the University of Arkansas while working in customer operations at an education technology start-up in Little Rock. Sara, her boyfriend Ben, and her cat Summer live in Chicago. She now works for a diversity hiring start-up based in NYC. Sara's grateful to be able to share her and her mom's story as part of *Truths We Tell* and recognizes the honor of sharing pages with the other storytellers.

Rick Chandler is boring. He is:

- old / boring
- married forever / boring
- retired / very boring but might beat working
- living in Missouri outside of Kansas City / boring, but good bbq
- father to two grown sons / they are not boring
- a storyteller who has told stories in ten different cities at the Moth Story Slam / not boring

Guy Choate learned to write when he joined the military as an Army journalist at the age of seventeen. He eventually earned his MFA at the University of New Orleans, where he wrote a thesis about being a good kid with what some people might call a gambling addiction. He's published essays in literary journals across the country, and last year Runaway Trolley Press published his first book, the illustrated essay "Gas! Gas! Gas!" He is founder and director of Argenta Reading Series in Little Rock, where he lives with his wife and two sons. Find him at guychoate.com.

Jennifer Tandy Cobb has built her career around telling other people's stories and is thrilled to now be sharing some of her own. She is the Executive Director of Donor Relations for University of Arkansas for Medical Sciences (UAMS) Institutional Advancement. Jennifer previously held leadership roles in strategic marketing at Arkansas Children's Hospital and at the Arkansas Children's Foundation. She also served as editor of *Little Rock Soirée* magazine and publisher/editor of *Little Rock Family* magazine. She holds a BA in English from Rhodes College. Jennifer is married to Chris Travis. Between them, they are the proud but exhausted parents of five teenagers and young adults.

Mackenzi Davis says, "Our voice is the most powerful tool we have. It is important and deserves space to be heard." Mackenzi finds a lot of joy in helping others find and promote their voice.

Ryan D. Davis is the director of UA Little Rock Children International, an international nonprofit organization that works toward significant and transformational change in the lives of children, youth, and families. Ryan is a native of Little Rock, where he serves on the boards of various justice and community-based organizations including Arkansas Public Policy Panel, Arkansas Coalition to Abolish the Death Penalty, DecARcerate Arkansas, Mosaic Templars Cultural Center (chair), and Arkansas Advocates for Children and Families (vice-chair). He is the treasurer for the Arkansas Freedom Fund. Ryan's writings have appeared in *Crisis Magazine*, *Black Books Bulletin*, *Arkansas Times*, *Sphinx*, *Stand News*, *The Chicago Defender*, and *Black Issues Book Review*. He is co-author of *Conversations in Color*. Ryan is an advocate for children, who represent the only future we have. He subscribes to the Kikuyu proverb "Work with the clay while it is still wet." Ryan is an ordained elder in the Christian Methodist Episcopal Church and the Associate Pastor at Bullock Temple C.M.E. Church. He is the grateful husband of Kimberly King Davis and father of Delaney, Sarah, and Ella.

Dr. Gloria Richard-Davis is Executive Director for University of Arkansas for Medical Sciences (UAMS) Division of Diversity, Equity, and Inclusion. She is a tenured Professor of Obstetrics and Gynecology, Division Director for Reproductive Endocrinology and Infertility, and Medical Director for the Physician Assistants program. She previously served as Professor and Chair of the Obstetrics and Gynecology Department at Meharry Medical College and Executive Director for Center for Women's Health Research (CWHR) from January 2007–2012. Gloria previously served as the Section Head of Reproductive Health Services for Ochsner Clinic Foundation and the Medical Director of the Fertility Center at Ochsner in New Orleans, and as Assistant Dean in Student Affairs and Assistant Professor in the Department of Obstetrics and Gynecology at Tulane University School of Medicine. Throughout her career, she has been a fierce supporter and advocate for diversity, equity, and inclusion. Much of her work in research has been focused on conditions that disproportionately affect women of color, such as fibroid. She has served on many boards focused on disparities, such as March of Dimes, Nashville CARES (an HIV nonprofit), and the National Medical Association Ob Gyn Executive Committee. She and her husband, Dr. Rodney Davis, have done multiple medical mission trips to eastern and western Africa—work they hope to continue in retirement.

Rev. Dr. Denise La Chelle Donnell is obsessed with the truth. She is a truth-seer, a truth-seeker, and a truth-teller. She devotes all of her time and energy to telling the truth about the truth. The truth about her bio is that none of the academic accomplishments it boasts have anything to do with her personal goals. Denise is an unwilling victim of various systems of oppression that have inadvertently positioned her to be one who can engage people from all walks of life in ways that are meaningful, significant, memorable, and transformative. Denise earned a BA in English from Jackson State University, a master's in secondary education from University of Mississippi, a master's in divinity from Perkins School of Theology, and a Ph. D. in Education Administration and Supervision from Jackson State University. When Denise is not engaged in conversations about the truth, she spends her time reading, writing, sketching, playing the piano, and throwing away all the food she cooks because it's too nasty to eat. You can find Denise live on Facebook at 9 a.m. Tuesday and Thursday mornings, hosting and co-hosting local community radio talk shows for KABF 88.3 FM, and Tuesday nights at 7 p.m. for Bible study.

Lynne Fay grew up in a military family and lived in two foreign countries and four states before graduating high school. She is now a professional writer who has worked in many fields of writing, including historical novels, literary scholarship, stage plays, radio copy, corporate communications, social media campaigns, and more. Her historical novels (published under a different name, Lynne Fay being a pen name) have won national awards and critical acclaim for their humanity, depth of research, and prose style. Lynne majored in theater as an undergraduate at Yale University and earned a master's in English from Emory University. She has performed her poetry on stage with the Arkansas Symphony Orchestra, has a passion for Shakespeare, and has appeared as an actor in the 2020 ACANSA Ten-Minute Play Showcase. Lynne is a lifelong nature lover who grew up singing to horses and riding bareback, and she still searches for unicorns when hiking in the woods.

David Fischman is an emergency medicine physician in beautiful Albuquerque, New Mexico. He spends his free time romping around the great outdoors with friends and loved ones, and once recharged, dedicates himself to the incredibly rewarding (though often demanding) job treating patients on the front line.

Bailey Gambill is an Arkansas native with an adventurous spirit. She completed her BA in English Literature from Arkansas State University and her master's in public administration from the University of Arkansas at Little Rock, and at the time of publishing is a law student at the William H. Bowen School of Law. She has used her story to help women in Asia escape sex trafficking, prostitution, and sexual assault. Currently, she serves as the Assistant Director of International Student Services at the University of Arkansas at Little Rock.

Raised in Hot Springs and a long-time resident of North Little Rock, **Karen Hayes** wrote poetry most of her life, but it wasn't until the death from Alzheimer's of her husband, Bobby J. Hayes, that she shared it with the public. Since then, Karen became a major force in the Arkansas poetry community, performing at venues throughout the state. She was known for her Poetry on Demand, using a 1971 manual Olivetti typewriter to write poems for people at events like the monthly Argenta Art Walk. She visited dementia wards and VA homes as a facilitator for the Alzheimer's Poetry Project, using poetry to connect with residents and caregivers. An avid runner, on her sixty-second birthday she ran sixty-two miles. Karen died unexpectedly January 31, 2019, with friends and family at her side. At the time of her death, Karen was working on an Alzheimer's book, a mix of memoir and poetry, which is scheduled for release in 2021.

Karen's story was read by **Mark Hotchkiss**, the "library guy" in her piece. Karen was the light of his life. A New England transplant, Mark is on staff at the Central Arkansas Library System's Main Library in Little Rock's River Market. Mark has performed in local theater and sings with the a cappella vocal quartet, Zirconium.

Nicole Hellthaler is the Assistant Director for Prison Yoga Project and a graduate of the Clinton School of Public Service and the University of Connecticut. In addition to developing, monitoring, and sustaining programs, she teaches weekly yoga classes at local juvenile and adult jails. She is also a yoga teacher for Barefoot Studio and a server at @ the Corner. While originally from Connecticut, Nicole has found home and community in Little Rock.

STORYTELLER BIOGRAPHIES

Emily Wernsdorfer Hooker is originally from Pennsylvania, but she has lived in Arkansas since 2008 and considers the South home now. Emily is the Associate Director at Ferncliff Camp & Conference Center, the perfect job for someone who loves spending time outdoors and working with children and youth. In her spare time, Emily enjoys hiking, traveling, reading, birdwatching, and knitting. As a supporter of The Yarn, Emily loves attending storytelling events to hear the lived experiences of those in her community. She lives in North Little Rock with her husband, Joseph, and dog, Butler.

Little rock native, **Meosha "Yosh" Howard** is the creator and organizer for Little Rock Queer Girls and Memphis Queer Girls. Both groups were created to cultivate a community for queer women in Little Rock, Memphis, and surrounding areas. She is also a licensed Esthetician and owner of Infidimensional Skin.

Rah Howard is a musician, artist, photographer, and videographer from Little Rock. His work has been featured on media outlets such as MTV.com, Shade 45 radio, Fox Business News, PBS, and more. He is extremely passionate about using his gifts to improve the world around him and make a positive impact in his community.

Kevin L. Hunt, Sr. is a native of Little Rock. He is the son of a very strong mother and father, and was influenced by his grandmother and great-grandmother. He is also the proud father of one son, Kevin L. Hunt, Jr., and the husband of the love of his life, Maggie F. Hunt. Kevin Hunt Sr. dropped out of school in junior high. His life went into a downward spiral for many years afterwards. Unable to support himself due to his lack of education, Kevin relied on his family for their financial support. In 2001, he made a decision that would be the catalyst for changing his entire life: he enrolled in the Shorter College GED program. After earning his GED, Kevin courageously enrolled in Philander Smith College, where he not only received a business degree, but graduated with honors. He went on to receive a master's degree from Webster University. Kevin is author of *Why Me God? "Because I Ordained Your Steps."* Kevin is founder of a program for highschoolers called "Lessons Learned" and the nonprofit "Inspiring Other People" and is the host of the *Your Voice, Your Reason* Podcast. He serves on the board for Arkansas Coalition of Juvenile Justice and The Watershed—the world's first social hospital, led by his mentor and spiritual father, Rev. Hezekiah Stewart.

Anna Kimmell is an actor, educator, and theatre artist from Atlanta. A graduate of Elon University with a BFA in Musical Theatre, she has performed across the country in regional productions at Rhode Island's Theatre by the Sea, Colorado's Lake Dillon Theatre, Virginia's Mill Mountain Theatre, Arkansas's Arkansas Repertory Theatre, Georgia's Georgia Shakespeare, Theatre of the Stars, and *The Wizard of Oz* National Tour, to name a few. As an educator, Anna specializes in musical theatre, acting, and dance curricula for students of all ages. She served as the Director of Education at Mill Mountain Theatre in Virginia from 2013–2016 and Arkansas Repertory Theatre in Little Rock from 2016–2020. Anna has also led theatre dance courses at Hollins University and the University of Central Arkansas and a series of theatre workshops for rural elementary students in Los Andes, Chile. She now lives in Asheville, North Carolina, and leads the education programs at Flat Rock Playhouse.

Lorenzo Lewis is a social entrepreneur, professional speaker, and founder of The Confess Project, an initiative that centers on mental health and wellness for young men of color. Born in jail to an incarcerated mother, Lorenzo struggled with depression, anxiety, and anger throughout his youth. At seventeen, after almost reentering the system of mass incarceration he had come from, he began his journey to wellness. In 2019 Lorenzo received the National Alliance on Mental Illness (NAMI) Multicultural Outreach Award and the American Psychiatric Association Award for Advancing Minority Mental Health, and he was a finalist for the Little Rock Regional Chamber Small Business Owner 30 & Under of the Year Award. In 2020, he became a fellow of both the Roddenberry and Echoing Green Foundations. Lorenzo has appeared in *O Magazine* (as one of eleven 2020 Health Heroes), Lady Gaga's Born This Way Foundation, Watch The Yard, and more. In March 2021, The Confess Project was listed by Fast Company as a "Top 10 Most Innovative Health Company." Since May 2016, The Confess Project has reached over thirty thousand individuals in thirteen cities and is currently partnering with Gillette to reach one million individuals nationwide.

STORYTELLER BIOGRAPHIES

Spencer Lucker Spencer Lucker is a community leader and passionate public servant who has dedicated his career to improving workforce and economic opportunity in underestimated communities. He was born, raised, and proudly educated in Little Rock, Arkansas, and the Mid-South, a region full of storytellers with plenty of stories to tell. As mentioned in his story, he is the proud son of two mothers to whom he credits his successes and the man he has grown to be. He now lives in Detroit, Michigan, with his wife, Stephanie, their twins, Avi and Mila, and their dog son, Cosmo.

Ryan McGeeney is a writer and photographer living in Little Rock. A native of Kansas, Ryan served in the U.S. Marine Corps before completing degrees in government and journalism. He has lived in Arkansas since 2009, where he has written about rural issues and agriculture. He is also a woodworker and, most insufferably, an ultrarunner. He occasionally has a drink or two.

Crystal C. Mercer is an Afro-Creative, Textile Artist, Actor, Activist, Poet and Author of *A Love Story Waiting to Happen* (Butterfly Typeface, 2018), Creative Director of Columbus Creative Arts + Activism, and Designer and Lead Merchant of Mercer Textile Mercantile. In her first children's book, *From Cotton to Silk: The Magic of Black Hair* (Et Alia, 2021), her expertise in sewing and textiles are on full display as its pages reveal 467 hours of hand-stitching. Crystal fuses arts and activism by using theatre and textiles to tell social justice narratives through merchandising and storytelling, with an emphasis on uplifting voices of color and making marginalized populations visible. Crystal is the recipient of grants from PEN America and the Dramatist Guild Foundation, which help her continue her charge as a storyteller and a keeper of the culture. She is a 2019 graduate of the Clinton School of Public Service (MPS) and completed her capstone and an international public service project in Accra, Ghana. She was emcee of the 2017 Women's March for Arkansas and regularly commands the stage as she reads her poetry in venues such as the Arkansas Black Hall of Fame. The daughter of legendary late civil rights lawyer, Attorney Christopher C. Mercer, Jr., she honors the legacy of her father by using artistic mediums as a tool for empowerment, education, and social justice. Find her at crystalcmercer.com and mercertextilemercantile.com.

LaTasha Moore is a native Arkansan from Falcon. She graduated from Prescott High School and earned bachelor's degrees in Spanish and Communication Studies from Arkansas State University. While there, she was awarded the prestigious R.E. Lee Wilson Award. In 2017, she earned a master's of public health from University of Arkansas for Medical Sciences (UAMS), and is currently completing a master's in Spanish from University of Central Arkansas. In 2018, LaTasha took her Spanish fluency skillset and created the education company Tasha Teaches Spanish. She and her staff work to "unite communities through language" and open the eyes, ears, and minds of native English speakers to the beauty of the Spanish language and those who speak it. LaTasha is also a poet who goes by the stage name Story.Tell.Her. She is married to IT professional and graphic artist Corey Coleman, and they have two sons, Khari and Khan Coleman.

Rick Owen grew up in Minneapolis but is now a Southerner, as he has lived in Little Rock for thirty years. He shares his life with his beautiful wife, Ann Owen, and was thrilled to become a grandfather several years ago. He loves the outdoors, volunteers for environmental causes, and makes music—he writes songs and plays acoustic and bass guitar. Rick is a psychiatrist by training and works at the Central Arkansas Veterans Healthcare System where he is the Associate Chief of Staff for Research. He has directed the VA Center for Mental Healthcare and Outcomes Research for twenty-two years, is a professor of psychiatry at the University of Arkansas for Medical Sciences (UAMS) Psychiatric Research Institute, and a professor of epidemiology in the College of Public Health. For nearly thirty years, he has conducted research to improve healthcare delivery and outcomes for individuals living with serious mental illness. He served on the National Alliance on Mental Illness (NAMI) Arkansas Board from 2007–2012.

Chauncey Holloman Pettis is the thirty-three-year-old CEO of Harlem Lyrics, LLC, and the Arkansas Women's Business Center Director for Winrock International. She is a mentor, public speaker, and community servant. Chauncey has over ten years of passion and expertise in the world of entrepreneurship and small business development. Harlem Lyrics, LLC, is a certified minority-owned business that was co-created in 2003 by Chauncey at the age of fifteen. As an integrated product line, Harlem Lyrics products included greeting cards, school supplies, and apparel. Since its inception, Harlem Lyrics' products have been sold in Kroger, Walgreens, Simply Fashions, It's Fashion, Borders Books, and Macy's.

Molly Reed has a degree in creative writing, which she puts to use for various businesses as a full-time freelance writer. She owns her own company, F. Reed Writing Co., writing website content, blogs, advertising copy, social media, commissioned short stories, and even custom love letters! She shared her story in The Yarn's "Love" show because she wanted to create something meaningful and relatable and that might reach others while expressing a little of her inner landscape. Basically, she wanted to see if she could still write for the joy of it. She had more fun diving into the process of writing, workshopping, and performing than she can adequately express, and she is so thankful to The Yarn for helping her tell her story. She hopes other queer people, people with moms, and people with friends who are queer and/or have moms take something positive away from it.

Robyn D. Rektor is a writer, editor, and teacher who enjoys sharing life experiences in articles and essays. She loves writing for the magic of turning a blank page into a story. She has spent most of her life in central Arkansas, except for a few years traveling and living on the East Coast, and is in the process of moving to the Ozarks. She loves reading, hiking, traveling, and volunteering.

Justin Sarlo is a Little Rock native who is active in many areas of the LGBT community and beyond. He has been involved in many charities, including PFLAG New Hampshire and Renegades for a Cause (as a founding member). Through Renegades for a Cause and on his own, he has assisted various organizations, including Arkansas AIDS Foundation, Arkansas Children's Hospital, Reach Out and the Christmas Caravan, Lucie's Place, and many others.

Andrea Toomer has six years of experience working in the ICU as a Registered Nurse. She graduated from University of Arkansas at Fayetteville with her Bachelor of Science in Nursing. She has been a traveling nurse working throughout the United States for over three years. She enjoys traveling, camping, hiking, and photography.

Glendaliz Torres is a mother to three talented and loving humans, a grandmother to six amazing grandchildren, and a wife to an incredible and very quiet man. Glendaliz loves being involved in her community and being of help to those in need, and enjoys working with multicultural populations and volunteering with organizations that aid immigrants in Little Rock. She has over twenty-five years of experience working with children and families. Glendaliz received her bachelor's degree in social work from the University of Arkansas in Little Rock and is working on a master's degree in social work from University of Arkansas at Little Rock and a Master of Public Service from the University of Arkansas Clinton School of Public Service. She has had many people in her life that have guided, supported, and inspired her. She strives to pay it forward every day to honor those who have helped in her life.

Andrew Vaught is the Hendrix Murphy Visiting Fellow in Theatre Arts at Hendrix College. He grew up in Covington, Louisiana, where he learned how to make theatre in a barn with a tin roof. And wasp nests. He was the co-founder and co-artistic director of the Cripple Creek Theatre Company, an anarcho-syndicalist performance troupe in New Orleans. He writes plays about monster truck drivers and unwise explorers and believes firmly in inanimate objects speaking their piece on the stage. He holds an MFA in creative writing from the University of New Orleans. He is grateful to The Yarn for building such a vibrant and welcoming community.

Jason Woods is associate director, writer, and editor for The Global FoodBanking Network. He grew up in Stillwater, Oklahoma, and now lives in Little Rock. For as long as he can remember, he's been fascinated by the supernatural. At The Yarn, Jason told the tale of what just might have been a run-in with a vengeful poltergeist in Edinburgh's most famous mausoleum.

CREATOR BIOGRAPHIES

HILARY TRUDELL, *Truths We Tell* curator, is a facilitator, producer, and educator with over fifteen years experience in the field of public service and the arts. She specializes in community engagement, arts education, and providing a platform for storytelling and advocacy work. Hilary currently works as the Director of Local Programming and Regional Outreach at the Clinton School of Public Service, leading first-year students through their first field work experience. Hilary has developed curricula on the topics of team building, community development, and advocacy through storytelling and is thrilled to be providing a platform to bring more Arkansas voices to the stage. Her past work includes supporting the production of Broadway-caliber shows at the Kennedy Center for Performing Arts, producing the Student Playwrights Project at Arena Stage, and supporting steering committees of volunteer leaders through the Human Rights Campaign. In 2017, Hilary founded The Yarn, whose mission is to amplify voices, build understanding, and create a space for human connection. As of August 2021, The Yarn is entering its fifth season, and Hilary and her team have produced over twenty shows. Since moving back to Arkansas in 2015, Hilary has personally coached over 250 people in efforts to help them share their stories succinctly, effectively, and with impact. In 2018, she also founded the ACANSA Ten-Minute Play Showcase, which she will usher into its fourth season in March 2022. A board member of the ACANSA Arts Festival, Hilary is a strong believer in leveraging stories as catalysts for community building, education, and social change.

JULIANNE DUNN, *Truths We Tell* production editor, is an educator, a program manager, and a facilitator. She loves a good story and believes in the power of sharing a person's or community's story to develop connection and to lead to understanding, collaboration, and innovation. She currently works as an Instructor of Economic Development at the University of Arkansas System Division of Agriculture in the Community, Professional, and Economic Development office. She previously worked as an operations consultant assisting business startups in the Washington, D.C. area and as the Assistant Director of Field Service at the UA Clinton School of Public Service, engaging community partners and helping students identify and implement successful field projects. She has an MA in public service from the Clinton School, an MA in public health from the University of Arkansas for Medical Sciences, and a BA in political science from the University of Missouri-Kansas City.

STACY COX, *Truths We Tell* and The Yarn stage photographer, is a professional photographer. When she's not off photographing landscapes in the national parks or a family's smiling faces, she combines her passion for photography and volunteering and donates her time and service to nonprofits.

CREATOR BIOGRAPHIES

ERIN WOOD, *Truths We Tell* editor and publisher, owns and directs Et Alia Press—a Little Rock-based "small press for big voices" publishing award-winning children's books and adult nonfiction with strong ties to Arkansas. She lives to read, write, edit, coach writers, and provide publishing consultations, and is most proud that her nine-year-old daughter—Et Alia's junior editor—spent the pandemic authoring over one hundred graphic novellas. Erin is author of *Women Make Arkansas*: *Conversations With 50 Creatives* and editor of and contributor to *Scars: An Anthology*, which features forty contributors on scars of the body. Her work has been a notable in *The Best American Essays,* nominated for a Pushcart Prize, and anthologized in *Stone Gathering*, and has appeared in *Scary Mommy*, *The Rumpus*, *Catapult*, *River Teeth's* "Beautiful Things," *Ms. Magazine's* Blog, and elsewhere. Erin has an AB in English from Duke University, a JD from Georgia State University College of Law, and an MA in professional and technical writing from University of Arkansas at Little Rock. Visit her at erinwood.com and etalia-press.com.

AMY ASHFORD, *Truths We Tell* cover and layout designer, has provided award-winning cover design and layout for Et Alia from her hometown of Baton Rouge, Louisiana, since 2017. She holds a BFA from Louisiana State University with a concentration in Printmaking. In addition, she has studied at SVA and Parsons in New York City. Projects for Et Alia include the interior layout and cover design for nearly every Et Alia book, including hand-illustration for the award-winning cover of *Can Everybody Swim? A Survival Story from Katrina's Superdome* and design for the award-winning cover of *Women Make Arkansas: Conversations with 50 Creatives.* Her other clients include specialty foods companies which fuel her passion for food and drink.

www.ingramcontent.com/pod-product-compliance
Lightning Source LLC
LaVergne TN
LVHW060620110826
845147LV00019B/1058

9781944528157